Shr

the News

Shrinking the News

Headline stories
on the couch

Coline Covington

KARNAC

First published in 2014 by
Karnac Books
118 Finchley Road
London NW3 5HT

British Library Cataloguing in Publication Data

A C.I.P. card for this book is available from the British Library

ISBN: 978–1–78220–095–6

Typeset by Vikatan Publishing Solutions (P) Ltd., Chennai, India

Printed in Great Britain

www.karnacbooks.com

CONTENTS

ABOUT THE AUTHOR

Coline Covington is a training analyst of the Society of Analytical Psychology and the British Psychotherapy Foundation. She is a member of International Dialogue Initiative (IDI), a group formed by Professor Vamik Volkan, Lord Alderdice, and Dr Robi Friedman to apply psychoanalytic concepts in understanding political conflict. Her publications include *Terrorism and War: Unconscious Dynamics of Political Violence* (Karnac, 2002) and *Sabina Spielrein: Forgotten Pioneer of Psychoanalysis*, second edition (Routledge, 2014). She is a regular columnist for *The Week* online.

PREFACE

In the autumn of 2008, I met Mark Law, the editor of the first UK online newspaper, *The First Post*. I asked him whether he might be interested in publishing a piece on the news from a psychoanalytic viewpoint. To my surprise, he said, "OK. Write something about Sarah Palin." Sarah Palin was then leading the Tea Party to dizzying and unexpected heights in the US electoral race, a curious phenomenon. My article on Palin appeared on 1 October 2008.

For two years, I wrote a regular column commenting on current events. *The First Post* has now become *The Week* online—a newspaper with a circulation of over two hundred thousand in the UK and abroad.

These fifty-eight articles from *The First Post/The Week* cover a range of subjects from political events to the wonders of stardom, from gruesome crimes that are hard to fathom to the bizarre trends that colour our daily lives. The topics were selected by me and my editors, depending on which headlines caught our attention at the time. We wanted to know why people do the things they do and what these events tell us about our unconscious behaviour—both individually and collectively.

Psychoanalysis makes people nervous. It is often considered mysterious; impossible to understand, because of its impossibly arcane language; and self-indulgent, making patients unnaturally dependent for years on end. Nor is the profession very good at making its ideas and practices understandable to the general public. In applying psychoanalytic ideas to current events, I hope in this book to make psychoanalysis more widely accessible.

The articles offer snapshots of some of the political and social preoccupations during the two-year period from 2008 to 2010, concluding with three more recent articles, from 2013. Many of the events covered were either caused by or set against the background of an economic recession that was to affect most of the globe. The balance of political power also changed radically in different parts of the world. But perhaps the greatest change is in the way electronic media now impinge on every aspect of our lives.

With increasing exposure to an ever-growing database of knowledge and experience, our social, political, and personal boundaries are expanding dramatically. As these articles reflect, everything is viewable at the press of a computer button—from wars to sex to dying. This must affect the way we think and behave: and in years to come, we may begin to comprehend just how we have changed. But whatever the future holds, our unconscious minds will continue to provide a mirror for our actions and guide the way we understand ourselves and the world around us.

I would like to give special thanks to my two editors, Mark Law and Nigel Horne, who have tutored me in the art of journalism and have been constant sources of inspiration and encouragement.

The articles are presented in chronological order with the date of posting on the internet cited at the end of each article.

Shrinking the News

1

Why Palin appeals to shell-shocked Americans

She is the perfect leader for Americans eager to apportion blame for the Wall Street crisis

In the immediate aftermath of 9/11, nearly every American house and apartment building flew the national flag, and US foreign policy became in some respects as nationalistic and isolationist as it had during the McCarthy era. This was the first attack that the US had suffered on home soil since Pearl Harbor, and Americans felt more vulnerable than ever before.

This vulnerability was only exacerbated by the fact that capturing Osama bin Laden and conquering the forces of al-Qaeda were simply not happening the way they were meant to.

In the past weeks, we have witnessed an even greater attack on the US in the form of the collapse of its financial markets. What were once considered "safe-as-houses" investments are now suddenly in the high-risk category. Humpty-Dumpty has indeed had a great fall.

As a result, the US is suffering from narcissistic shell-shock. When the over-confident individual suffers a life blow that is beyond his control, his first response is usually to attempt to regain an illusion of control by blaming the "other", whomever that "other" might be. Then, as a consequence of projecting blame onto others, the individual becomes paranoid about anything "other" or foreign, and this in turn can be used to justify further attacks. Finally, he retrenches into the stronghold of narcissistic behaviour and its promise of safety in power.

Because the financial crisis has been spawned from within the US, and not by outside enemies, it is trickier to deal with than 9/11. The "blame" is much harder to push onto "others". One way of dealing with this kind of internal disaster/attack is by treating it as a kind of tsunami, or a phenomenon that is beyond our control and in the hands of God, nature, or fate.

Who could be better at spearheading this approach than Sarah Palin, McCain's choice as vice-presidential candidate? She has deliberately perpetrated the image of the frontierswoman at a time when it is bound to be most appealing to members of a country that feels itself to be fighting against all the odds and that is anxious not only about losing ground (and face) but about what might be coming over the next hill.

The frontier spirit is just what is needed. The American Indians have been replaced by the Iraqis, ecological concerns have been wiped off the slate altogether under the "hand of God" approach, while the collapse of the financial markets can be understood as a temporary blip that simply needs tweaking to ensure continuing belief in a free-market economy.

Behind her policies, there is an assumption, as in the days of the American frontier, that there are endless possibilities for conquest, a wilderness with a surfeit of wildlife in no need of protection, and endless national resources to be tapped so that Americans can continue to drive huge cars on endless motorways, use air conditioning in the summer and winter, and get fat on a limitless supply of hamburgers and fake foods.

This belief in the bounty of the US is reassuring to say the least. When bounty fails and it is attributed to fate, this is also reassuring. The narcissist does not need to question his own role in destructiveness or as the cause of any problems; he can confer these neatly on to others or other reasons that do not incur his responsibility.

Most important, the narcissist does not need to accept limitations; he can remain omnipotent and maintain the illusion that he is at the centre of the world. This is very reassuring when things aren't going so well, but it also has the unfortunate side effect of fostering paranoia.

Freud first came up with the idea of the "narcissism of minor differences" in 1918 when he was writing about sexual difference and extended this idea to encompass the paranoia and hatred that can emerge most fiercely among neighbours in times of crisis. Freud makes the link between narcissism and intolerance explicit in his 1930 essay *Civilisation and Its Discontents*, in which he explains our aversion towards strangers as a defensive function, or as a form of narcissism, in the service of self-preservation.

We try to ensure our self-preservation by projecting our aggression into the "other", whether it is an individual or a group, so we can remain protected from it. When the crisis is within, the "stranger" is found within the group, creating a split between the good and bad, the powerful and the weak.

A consequence of the current financial crisis is that voters are now targeting Wall Street bankers as the new enemy within. Blame is not shared, nor is responsibility; it is pushed onto the "other".

We can see Palin rising like Athena from Zeus's brow ready to enter into battle to preserve the narcissism of the nation. She aims to maintain the purity of the frontier and the people by attacking the scientists, the educators, the politicians, and the economists— and let's not forget the ecologists—who threaten the frontier movement by pointing out its limitations and its hazards.

1 October 2008

2

The danger of a banker with a power complex

The "do-something" culture of the financial world is ill-equipped to deal with panic

There is no petrol in the state of Tennessee. And for the first time in four years, the Dow Jones has fallen below the critical 10,000 mark. In London, too, shares fell yesterday to a four-year low. In short, panic has set in with the result that people are buying feverishly or not at all.

Our word "panic" comes from the Greek god Pan, the herdsman, who was famous for being able to inspire fear and disorder among people. The Olympian victory over the assault of the Titans was attributed to Pan's power to create a "panic". Whoever falls under the spell of a "panic" is in serious trouble.

The collapse of the financial markets has created a world-wide panic with inevitable repercussions. Even those who may be relatively untouched by what is going on have cause to worry. Individuals and institutions express their panic in one of two ways, with strikingly similar effects. There is the lemming-like behaviour in which, pressed to survive, the individual will carry on regardless of the circumstances, continuing to be active until he has actually jumped off the cliff into the icy waters to reach the other side. A perilous decision but one that is, ironically, in keeping with the way many financial institutions are run. In retrospect, Lehman Brothers' plummet seems to fall into just this kind of category.

There is a well-established ethos in the City that is at the core of free-market capitalism and that is to be active, to produce, to acquire, to grow, to be in control. In short, it is to be powerful. The ones who get to the top are often, or at least so the mythology goes, the ones who are most driven and ruthless and, significantly, most active. They do more deals, make more money, and increasingly take more risks. We are now seeing this spiral unravelling with a trajectory just as breathtaking as its rise.

When those who are most driven and who are most anxious about staying in control face imminent danger, the reaction is more often than not to *do* something—in other words, to continue to drive on even harder. There are plenty of examples of investors who suddenly pull out of their rapidly dwindling investments and gamble on dark horses and back runners, only to lose the lot. They wave their arms around to show how much they are achieving in the midst of a crisis, and we can see many of them waving their arms as they race towards the cliff's edge and fall off. In fact, it makes one wonder whether all this phallic behaviour has not been a major contributing factor in what may be the demise of capitalism as we know it.

The other reaction we are witnessing is perhaps more subtle but every bit as destructive. This is the individual who feels that the collapse of the market reflects his own failure and ineptitude and who voluntarily offers himself as a sacrificial lamb on the altar of financial recovery. Or, in other words, in anticipation of being laid off, this is the individual who offers to resign. We could call this the "inverse lemming" position.

The lemming in the first instance tries to allay his fears and those of others by becoming even more active in the deluded idea that he can reverse the trend by running even harder. The inverse lemming, on the other hand, is equally omnipotent in his thinking, but this takes the form of overwhelming responsibility and guilt that can only be alleviated by diving over the cliff, but this time by walking backwards.

Fortunately, not everyone in the financial world behaves like lemmings. There are some who manage to keep their heads amid the panic and lie in wait without having to *do* something to prove they are potent. But this is a position that requires a certain degree of passivity, which in itself is antithetical not only to the culture concerned but also extremely hard to maintain in the face of an adrenaline rush.

Being passive does not mean doing nothing. It means keeping a space open in our minds to observe what is happening and to think until the time is right to act. Then we can engage with the crisis rather than being driven to the brink by it, as captives of Pan.

7 October 2008

3

Frieze Art Fair: artistic or autistic?

Symptoms of autism among the Frieze artworks

Entering the huge Frieze Art Fair pavilion in Regent's Park, you hear the sound of trickling water, an installation by Pavel Bucher. This is the first clue that nature and the environment are going to feature as a noticeable theme this year. But what is surprising is the particular way in which the environment is perceived and portrayed.

There are numerous examples of actual environments that have been re-assembled into art installations. The most striking is the Icelandic exhibit of an art bar, Sirkus, taken lock, stock, and barrel from Reykjavik by the gallery Kling and Bang and re-assembled next to the Caprice food concession.

Sirkus is a bar run by artists that opened in 1987 and recently closed. The structure and its contents, including barman and performance artists, have been faithfully re-created, and there is a long queue of fair-goers waiting to go in. The gallery claims that it has managed to create the environment of the original bar but in a different context. Nevertheless, this bar is for sale at £350,000, not including transport or VAT.

There are other examples of environments that have been similarly "airlifted" into the fair: a rubbish dump from the Appetite

Gallery in Buenos Aires, with the artists rummaging through the garbage; a man in a suit—from the Fair Gallery—standing with a sign-board hung around his chest saying, "Help me to Find a Wife".

While these installations have a humorous side, they came across like a pack of tourist postcards, simply replicating different environments and experiences. Rather than invite you into a world of fantasy and feeling, they distance the viewer from experiencing the actual threat our environment is under. So much so, that after several turns around Frieze, I began to feel I was surrounded by autistic objects in an autistic world.

In child development, autism is a normal state of mind in infancy in which pleasure is sought through bodily sensations, and objects in the external environment are used for this purpose and are not perceived as having a life of their own. It is a state of omnipotence over the environment that obliterates separation and relationship.

Autism becomes abnormal when an infant needs to defend himself against being left too much alone to cope with the hazards of the environment. This is experienced as a traumatic separation and loss. Then the infant retreats into a sealed-off world in which he tries to re-create this earlier sense of omnipotence.

It is a sensual world totally within his control. The environment is nothing more than a collection of objects, stripped of meaning except for the sensual pleasure they may give. This is why children and adults who suffer from autism are so impenetrable and so hard to relate to.

As well as the "airlifted" installations, environmental awareness is evident at Frieze in other pieces such as a water condensation chamber, constructed by the artist Tue Greenfort, that siphons off body moisture emitted by the fair-goers into plastic water bottles; a photograph of dead skinned bears nailed to a plank from the Moscow gallery Regina; a video of rats packed into a glass container trying to claw their way out, from another Moscow gallery, XL.

While these are all striking, and in some cases repellent, pieces, their conception is so concrete that they verge on the kitsch. But while it might be easy to classify them as merely ineffectual or "bad" art, seen together they convey something more disturbing to do with a desire to possess and control the environment so that it is reduced to an object, becoming two-dimensional.

Could this be a response to our increasing awareness of the lack of control we have over our environment, and to our fear of what we have already destroyed? Or is this an "autistic" response— an attempt to freeze time and space so that nothing can change or impinge on us or our worldview?

In the midst of the many two-dimensional objects and installations at Frieze, there are notable exceptions. The piece that seemed to stand out as a true expression of the pain and isolation of an autistic world was a sculpture by Anselm Kiefer, titled *Paete non dolet* ("She who cannot be touched does not grieve"), from White Cube.

The sculpture, made of plaster of Paris and fabric, shows a woman draped in a wedding dress, much like a caryatid, with a tangled cluster of barbed wire in place of her head. The juxtaposition of the inviting drapes surrounding the woman's body and the barbed, impenetrable mental space portrays the painful conflict of being trapped within one's own defences to the point of becoming a lifeless object.

The sculpture was in fact removed by Saturday morning because too many people had become caught up in the barbed wire and had complained of being attacked. The paradox of autism?

20 October 2008

4
The new feminism: how Michelle Obama is changing the rules

Michelle Obama is a feminist success story: she is mother of two, she's graduated from two of the most prestigious universities in the US (Princeton and Harvard) and practises as a lawyer, she's a loyal, supportive wife who is also her husband's best advisor and critic, she speaks her mind and has moved the nation with her convention speech, and she is never away from home more than two nights running.

Even her wardrobe smacks of style and sense, preferring the relatively affordable chic of young American designers to haute couture—a political statement that is not lost on young American voters.

She is also African-American and her experience of racism— more than sexism—is undoubtedly an important link between her and her husband and their shared vision of a plural society.

She has been compared with Jackie Kennedy, Hillary Clinton, and Cherie Blaire, and yet there is something unmistakably different about her from any of her predecessors or European counterparts. She represents, particularly for the generation of young women in their twenties and thirties in the US who are starting careers and families, a role model that we have never seen before in the political arena.

Historically, black women in the US have more often than not been single heads of the family and are used to being in charge. Michelle Obama breaks both the stereotype of a black woman on her own and that of a white woman who is an appendage of her husband. She is a wife but she is also an equal to her husband. In the US, this is a more radical change than it may seem at first sight.

Women's image in the US (and in Britain) changed radically in the 1920s with the vote and the effects of the First World War. A decade later, a new feminine archetype had begun to form in the American psyche. She was a tough, independent, brainy, and sexy woman. In Hollywood, she was epitomised by Katherine Hepburn, Bette Davis, and Joan Crawford.

By the start of the Second World War, we see the likes of the comic-book heroine Lois Lane, fellow reporter and love interest of Clark Kent (aka Superman), come on the scene. These were strong, independent women with minds of their own, but they were not usually portrayed as married or as being mothers. Lois Lane did eventually marry Superman—but not until 1996 (a fifty-eight-year courtship!) and never had children.

These Athena-type women fought for patriarchal values, smoked and drank with the men, but had no real power in a man's world and no real potency in a woman's world. Having brains and being a maternal woman did not co-exist.

American feminism first really challenged this split in the 1960s, partly as a reaction to the Baby Boom years of the 1950s in which women were pushed out of the workplace back into the home. The new feminists called for equality on every level between men and women, and attacked the idea of difference between the sexes. Sexual difference was vilified as the root of women's subjugation.

While this radical feminist position has been significantly modified over the last forty years or so, it has left in its wake a lot of confusion about what it means to be a "real woman" and, for that matter, a "real man". What used to be clearly proscribed gender roles have now been thrown up in the air, and there is a great deal of uncertainty between the sexes as to how to treat each other, much less how one wants to be treated.

Amidst this confusion, a lot of young American women seem to think that feminism is primarily about sticking up for other women. One of the striking things about Hillary Clinton's campaign was that so many of the young women who were asked why they were voting for Clinton answered that it was "because she is a woman". When asked about the policies she supported, these women often had no idea—and no awareness of how sexist their response was!

Michelle Obama seems to have steered her way through this feminist morass with remarkable grace. She stands for a more mature feminism in which women no longer need to rebel against men and compete to be the same as men, as happened during feminism's adolescence.

Perhaps all those years in which women have been struggling to have their masculine side valued have begun to pay off. Women are now freer to value men (with their feminine side), and this in turn frees women to express their femininity and to value their more traditional roles as wives and mothers at the same time.

The feminism that is emerging is more sophisticated and nuanced, and, most importantly, more able to encompass diversity—be it gender or race or simply different viewpoints. As a couple, the Obamas are a shining example of how men and women can help and respect each other, work together as equals, and raise children as partners, with differences that strengthen the family and enrich society.

If Jerry Siegel and Joe Shuster, the inventors of Superman and Lois Lane, were alive today, they would surely applaud, if not anticipate, this new version of Lois Lane—crack investigative reporter, mother of two, and devoted wife, who knows when to keep her mouth shut and can sniff the dreaded Kryptonite a mile off. The "real woman" at last.

1 November 2008

5

For glamour models, sex
is in the eye of the camera

Girls these days, according to writer Natasha Walter, are no longer looking for love. Casual sex is cool. As one sixth-form girl bragged, "I don't have boyfriends. I have sex with men, but I wouldn't call them boyfriends." Natasha Walter has put her finger on the pulse in her new book, *Living Dolls*, to be published next month.

What is being heralded as the new feminism by some young women—being as free as men have been in the past to be promiscuous without social stigma—is being seen by others as simply a form of sexism that denigrates women under the guise of political correctness. In other words, what men can do, women can do. Fair is fair. But is the new promiscuity amongst young women really about sex or is it a lust for fame?

Leading the trend at the hard end are the glamour models. These are young women who pose semi-naked for men's magazines, fashion shows, sports events, corporate events, television chat shows, and the list goes on. They typically start their careers on the internet, posting suggestive photographs of themselves and citing talents in acting or music.

"It's not just about tits, it's about personality too", as one disc jockey promoter claimed. Young women can be discovered online by agents and lured into modelling jobs that are progressively exploitative. Each pay rise is accompanied with the demands of exposing more nudity along with increasing pressure to sculpt the body into a more sexually desirable shape. The distinction between agent and pimp is often hard to make.

Walter describes disco scenes of "Babes on the Bed" competitions—that take place across the country—in which the winner gets a modelling contract with *Nuts* magazine. Semi-naked young women bounce up and down on a huge bed while men and women surround them, cheering them on and taking photos with their mobile phones. It is not very different from a striptease but arguably without the artistic performance. The DJ may direct the girls to kiss or fondle each other as a way of raising the excitement levels in the audience. The winner may also provoke girls into suggestive poses. One winner, Cara Brett, admonished a contestant, saying, "If you're going to be a glamour model, you've got to get your boobs out." It is clear that whatever sex is involved is purely voyeuristic.

While many of the young women, such as sixth-formers, whom Walter cites boast double figures of the sex they've had with different men, the would-be glamour models will also admit that what is most important to them is their careers. Glamour modelling is seen as the first step towards stardom. Using their bodies to achieve fame is their primary aim. These women, perhaps like their less ambitious but equally promiscuous sisters, are not driven by hormones so much as an intense need for narcissistic gratification. The object of their desire is not in fact a man or the pleasure they can derive from men, but their own bodies. Sexual excitement is sought from being seen as having a desirable body and "scoring" sexual conquests is merely one aspect of this.

For the glamour model, her body becomes a fetishistic object, imbued with all of the ingredients of a love object but with the added advantage being that it is in her possession and, as such, within her control. The sexual components of the body are exaggerated—lips, breasts, buttocks are noticeably enhanced—and the body becomes a sexual icon to be worshipped and emulated. In this respect, the body of the glamour model takes on the phallic qualities that were once attributed to powerful men. In treating their bodies as sexual objects, these young women have replaced their emotional need for a sexual partner with a narcissistic fixation on their own bodies. This is women's liberation at its most extreme. Who needs love when there is fame?

Freud might also have attributed this form of fetishism to women's disavowal of the fact that they don't have a penis, because this lack is perceived to be too painful and shameful to accept. In other words, it is too painful for young women to accept their need for another when this is something that they have experienced as shameful and humiliating.

Walter's hypothesis is that more young women today come from broken homes and identify with mothers who have been left alone and vulnerable by their male partners. While this explanation may account for a lack of trust in relationships, it does not explain the extreme narcissism that underlies this behaviour. Were these young women in some way treated as adored objects by their depressed mothers and are now treating their bodies in a similar way?

If it is true that young women are eschewing relationships and intimacy in favour of sex without attachment, this suggests that women are becoming more narcissistic and, ironically, more vulnerable to exploitation. Erica Jong introduced the ideal of the "zipless fuck". But the glamour model goes a step further with the ideal of the "photo fuck". The relation with camera/voyeur takes precedence over a relation with a real person, in this case a man. Casual sex can also be used to fuel the voyeuristic fantasy.

Nevertheless, it is reassuring that this is not every young woman's dream. As one contestant to the Babes in Bed competition admitted when the competition was over, "It was a bit degrading to be honest."

11 January 2009

6

Financial failure is simply the final, fatal blow

Insurmountable anger, not losing millions, is often the determining factor in suicide cases linked to debt

How many more victims of the financial crisis will there be? The US, the UK, Japan, India, and Egypt have all reported growing concern over suicides linked to debt. They are wise to be worried: in Japan, the suicide rate increased by thirty-four per cent during the 1998 financial crisis.

On the face of it, it is hardly surprising that a sudden downturn in an individual's finances can precipitate depression and, in certain cases, suicide. But what is most striking about many of the suicides reported here and in the US in the last few months is their extreme rage. Men who have lost their fortunes kill themselves and sometimes their families as well; wives kill themselves when their husbands lose everything; men and women kill themselves as their houses are repossessed.

These suicides may appear to be fuelled by despair, helplessness, shame, and, in some cases, guilt, but in many cases the suicide note reveals overwhelming anger. One woman, facing foreclosure on her house, wrote to the mortgage company: "You have failed to protect me. You have broken your promise. You have destroyed my life."

Mortgage companies, banks, investment companies, and now governments are being blamed by many people for their devastating losses. Since they can't murder the institutions or the Madoffs of this world, people are killing themselves instead. The Italian poet Cesare Pavese coined the phrase "suicides are shy homicides". Recent suicides linked to the financial crisis are no exception.

But it is not simply the case that people who have suffered these huge financial losses feel angry, let down, and helpless. For many of these suicides, financial failure is the final blow in a long history of feeling inadequate, rejected, and robbed of love. The murder that takes place is against an internal parental figure who has made the individual believe that he can only be loved if he is successful; more often than not, this also means being self-reliant and hard-working.

So, when financial loss occurs, it is especially traumatic. The efforts to gain love in the eyes of the parent have been suddenly wiped out in one fell swoop, and further efforts seem utterly futile. There is a powerful sense that everything is doomed to fail because it will all be undone in the end. Being left with no money, or no house, is equivalent to being left with a parent who has withdrawn love for no apparent reason.

More specifically, it is like being let down by a parent who puts their own needs first, leaving the child at risk. What seemed safe and relatively secure no longer exists, and the failure of the banks and mortgage companies to go on providing this security inevitably triggers off memories of parental failure that can feel life-threatening.

In some cases, the parent who needs to be pleased may also be projected onto the wife or husband, and the experience of rejection may thus be twofold. Failing one's spouse can be humiliating and shameful but also persecuting. One banker, referring to a colleague's suicide, described it as an act of honour because his colleague had felt so responsible to his clients for inadvertently losing their money in the Madoff fraud.

The guilt and despair such failure elicits is enormous. But so is the rage. In the case of people who have traumatic histories of emotional insecurity, the combination of despair and rage can produce a fatal cocktail. Add to this the impotence in not being able to actually kill the parent who has failed you (that is, the person or institution on whom you depended and who has betrayed you), and you come up with suicide.

19 January 2009

7

Don't bank on the buffalo: why we need to adapt or die

The need for people to reinvent themselves has never been so great. But can we do it?

A patient of mine—an ex-banker—recently professed that he didn't know who to be any more because his long-term vision of being a successful, rich, powerful banker was no longer possible. He is not alone: many of his peers are having an identity crisis.

Gone are the days when it was possible to make it rich with a click of the fingers and when bonuses alone were enough for families of five to live on for years—the ideal many recent city recruits were striving for. Now, not only have the pots of gold gone into negative equity, but the phones barely ring any more. What do you do when the conditions for a form of "success", for example making money, cease to exist? What happens to a culture?

In *Radical Hope*, a fascinating study of the demise of the Native American Crow tribe's way of life, Jonathan Lear examines what it takes to keep hope for the future alive. At the age of nine, the last great Crow chief, Plenty Coups, had a dream that there would be no more buffalo and that his people would fall to the ground and nothing more would happen.

Plenty Coups had his dream in 1857, and it correctly predicted the tribe's future: the Crow were hunters and, as the buffalo were wiped out, so was their way of life. But Plenty Coups had also had a dream that told him to be like the bird, the chickadee, and to listen to and learn from his environment. Thanks to the way they interpreted that dream, the Crow were able in subsequent years to settle their disputes peacefully with the whites.

What was significant about this dream was that it gave Plenty Coups and the members of his tribe a new way of being, a new cultural identity that enabled them not only to survive—the Crow Indians did far better in their negotiations over lands and rights with the US government than most other Indian tribes—but to construct a new vision of life that held hope. Lear argues that this can happen when a person or a group can transform their ego-ideal so that it can be congruent within a changed set of circumstances.

The idea of the ego-ideal goes back to Freud, and it constitutes a model to which the person aspires to conform. The Crow Indians' collective ego-ideal was bound up with being good hunters and fighters: when hunting is no longer possible and fighting over territory that is already demarcated has lost its purpose, this creates a crisis of meaning. Different options are then available, and we have seen the tragic results of many of them.

One miserable option is simply to survive materially and physically without hope. The effects of this option are all too evident in the Indian tribes who have been sequestered in reservations and are now suffering from serious depression, with alcoholism and crime rates rising.

An alternative option is that of carrying on with the old ideal in the name of honour—the kamikaze option—which was Sitting Bull's preference. As leader of the Sioux tribe, his strategy was to go on fighting the white man, a strategy that cost him and many others their lives.

Another option is to become assimilated into a new culture, though this can be at the risk of taking on a false or foreign identity that has not developed from within and fosters an unstable, *ersatz* culture. Since the credit crunch, job applications for the civil service "fast stream" have increased by more than thirty per cent and the education sector has seen a similar surge in applications. While these are considered "secure" jobs, it will be interesting to see how the ethos within these sectors is affected by a new group of employees—employees who may be coming with the mindset of "get rich quick" bankers.

Plenty Coups's achievement, at least according to Lear, was that he could hold out an ego-ideal to the Crow that embraced resilience and learning, receptivity and intelligence, instead of the old ideal of power obtained through success in the hunt and at war. Through this shift in ego-ideal, the Crow were able to recover a system of values and meaning and self-esteem which helped them to adapt within a new culture without losing their identity.

Is there a lesson we can learn from Plenty Coups now? For my ex-banker, and for us all, we need to face this fundamental question and to re-evaluate our values and our dreams.

28 January 2009

8

How can an Oxbridge Bishop deny the Holocaust?

**Bishop Williamson's Holocaust denial is a defence
strategy whose target is his own weaknesses**

Bishop Richard Williamson, averting his eyes from his interviewer,
solemnly claimed: "I believe there were no gas chambers."

How can a Cambridge-educated Bishop, conversant with the
ways of the world, deny that Jews were killed in gas chambers
during the Holocaust?

Bishop Richard Williamson, ex-communicated along with
three other Roman Catholic bishops twenty years ago for
belonging to the ultra-conservative Society of St Pius X, which
challenged the liberal reforms of the Second Vatican Council, did
just this in an interview on Swedish television last month.

He also reduced the figure of six million Jews killed in the
camps to "at most 300,000". It takes only a small amount of
research to find out where the Bishop got his "facts" from—
countless fringe historians offer alternative Holocaust accounts
on the internet. But what is puzzling is why a man in such a position would give precedence to these "facts" when the overwhelming evidence tells a very different story.

Freud defines denial as "a mode of defence which consists in
the subject's refusing to recognise the reality of a traumatic perception". In effect, the Bishop was saying: "It wasn't as bad as the Jews

have made it out to be." He pours fuel on the fire by saying he has studied the evidence, emphasising: "I'm not going by emotion."

So, in Bishop Williamson's view, the Jews and their sympathisers are not only exaggerating, they are *emotional* and therefore cannot be trusted.

On the face of it, this is exactly the kind of statement that a bully or an abuser makes about his victim: "Oh, I didn't hurt you, it wasn't that bad, stop being such a cry baby!" The bully despises weakness of any kind and projects his own failings and vulnerability on to others whom he can then hate and persecute.

It's a divide-and-rule policy in which what is thought to be "bad" is pushed into the "other", so that it can be controlled and ultimately eradicated—at least, that's the idea. Hitler located his own inadequacies in the Jews—the "foreigners"—and the disabled, and sought to purify himself by means of their extermination.

It is clear that the bugbear for the Bishop is "emotion", and the Jews seem to be the ones who are cursed with it. This may explain why the Bishop has a case of selective denial: he does not deny that Jews died in the camps, but his particular denial is aimed at accusing the Jews of being liars and being emotional. So the victims' stories are not to be trusted and the persecutors are not so bad after all. What's all the fuss about?

Bullies often become bullies because they have been bullied or abused themselves. This is called "identification with the aggressor" and is a way of splitting off and denying a traumatic experience. The surest way to survive the Mafia, for example, is to become a member.

But bullies also tend to suffer from paranoia, just like the Mafiosi, and with good reason. The Bishop concludes his interview by saying: "There's certainly been a huge exploitation. Germany has paid out billions and billions of deutsche marks, and now euro, because the Germans have a guilt complex about their having gassed six million Jews." "But I don't think six million Jews were gassed. Now be careful, I beg of you", looking the interviewer in the eye, "this [to deny the Holocaust] is against the law in Germany. If there were a German here", pointing over his shoulder, "you could have me thrown into prison before leaving Germany." Then, joking, "I hope that's not your intention!"

Is the bully Bishop showing signs of nervousness that his own internal Gestapo might turn the tables and he will become the one who is persecuted?

The real problem about denial is that because it requires the mind to split off bits of reality, there is a natural fault line that makes the whole system unstable. There are different ways out of this problem. Either the bully can have a psychotic breakdown, in which case reality goes out of the window, or the bully has to try to become even more powerful in order to keep his mental state intact.

It is the latter option that is the most dangerous. As Gregory H. Stanton, founder and president of Genocide Watch, warns us, "Denial is the eighth stage that always follows a genocide. It is among the surest indicators of further genocidal massacres. The perpetrators of genocide dig up the mass graves, burn the bodies, try to cover up the evidence and intimidate the witnesses. They deny that they committed any crimes, and often blame what happened on the victims."

Not only has Pope Benedict XVI recently rehabilitated Bishop Williamson back into the Vatican fold, but he has just promoted Austrian priest Father Gerhard Maria Wagner to bishop. Bishop Wagner is most well known for his declaration four years ago that Hurricane Katrina was God's "divine retribution" against the sexual permissiveness abounding in New Orleans.

He pointed to the fact that the hurricane had targeted nightclubs, brothels, and even abortion clinics as evidence that God was waging war against the sins of homosexuality, prostitution, and abortion. What is so extraordinary about this appointment is that it reveals such a literal, fundamentalist interpretation of natural events and such an anthropomorphic view of God. Is God really like a Father in the sky, looking over us and occasionally sending down thunder bolts when we misbehave?

Apart from the obvious question as to what the Pope thinks he's doing by seemingly endorsing such a politically incorrect view of the world, we must also ask whether there is some strain of paranoia that has infected some in the Vatican.

As with the case of Bishop Williamson, there is a whiff of anxiety that is being projected onto the usual fall guys out there—for Williamson, it is the Jews; for Wagner, it is the promiscuous (and homosexuals in particular). The extreme clampdown and imagined Godly attack against homosexuality suggests that it is a matter of considerable fear, desire (repressed or otherwise), and guilt within the ranks of the Church.

For Bishop Wagner, God performs the role of a super-ego outraged—and threatened—by the idea of sexuality gone wild. This tells us quite a bit about the repressed unconscious of the Church today.

3 February 2009

9

Roman Abramovich and Chelsea: it's all dad's fault

The Chelsea owner appears to be motivated in business dealings by feelings of abandonment

Another Chelsea Football manager bites the dust under the reign of Roman Abramovich. First, there was Claudio Ranieri, then Jose Mourinho, then Avram Grant, and now Luiz Felipe Scolari, each of them an expensive mistake.

The Russian billionaire has spent roughly £600 million on Chelsea since he acquired it in 2003. Why is he pouring all this money into a football club—and why can't any of the managers get it right, at least in the eyes of Abramovich?

His other spending habits—building an art collection with works by Bacon, Freud, and Giacometti, and helping his twenty-six-year-old girlfriend Dasha Zhukova open her contemporary art gallery in Moscow—suggest a midlife crisis. Or is there something more complex going on?

A snapshot biography of Abramovich reveals that his mother died when he was one and his father was killed when he was three. Terrible losses for a small child to endure.

He was then taken care of by two uncles and his grandmother in various households, not doing particularly well in school but finding his feet as an entrepreneur when he married his first wife, Olga, in 1987 and invested her parents' wedding present in black-market goods. This investment tripled in value.

This was the beginning of his meteoric business career and undoubtedly gave Abramovich not only the heady taste of power but also, and perhaps more importantly, the illusion that money can protect against loss. Because it is loss that Abramovich seems to be so anxious about.

Abramovich seems to have a habit of firing wives (he has been married twice) and football managers. It would not be surprising on either front if he were looking for his lost parents, the idealised and missing mother of his infancy, who can never be brought back to life, and the father on whom he depended and who also abandoned him in death.

Just as Abramovich's father failed to protect his son against the loss of his mother, no football manager can protect the team against loss. Scores count and losses count more.

Abramovich is emotional about the game and may well experience the team as an extension of himself. Perhaps he keeps hoping that he can find another father who can make things right for him and for the family?

He appoints a new father-manager, fires him, appoints another, and so on. In this way, the loss of the father is under Abramovich's control; he calls the shots and is not the one who is left, suddenly and traumatically.

It also means that the father-manager, once idealised, is doomed to fail when the team is not invincible. The father-manager plays the role of the scapegoat who, in his inevitable human weakness, comes to represent the vulnerability that Abramovich may be so frightened of within himself. Traditionally, the scapegoat is the willing victim that is sacrificed to restore and renew the powers of the ruler.

The problem is that as Abramovich becomes increasingly anxious about loss, the more heads are likely to roll. This in turn is likely to make Abramovich feel guilty—at least unconsciously—about getting rid of his managers, and possibly his wives as well.

He will then need to spend even more money on the next round in order to alleviate his guilt and win back the love he fears he has lost. This is an action re-play that no one wants to watch.

10 February 2009

10
Why Tzipi Livni craved the danger of a spy's double life

The Israeli prime ministerial wannabe saw parallels with the double lives her parents led

Working for Mossad, the Israeli intelligence service, was like "living constantly in two worlds". These were Tzipi Livni's words to describe her life as a twenty-two-year-old working undercover in a chic quarter of Paris in the early 1980s at the height of Israel's war with Lebanon.

In an interview circulated last week by Yediot Aharanot, originally published in a censored version fourteen years ago, Livni explains, "You're loaded up all the time with adrenaline. Most of the time I was doing strange things normal people never do. I lost all my spontaneity. You must be focused and calculated all the time. Even when I went to the newsagent I would check to see if I had a tail."

Livni only lasted a few years in Mossad before she left in 1984, when she married and launched her dazzling career in politics. Now aged fifty, negotiating to form a coalition that would make her Israel's first female prime minister since Golda Meir, her patriotic past with Mossad has been conveniently revisited in what looks like an effort to boost her reputation.

Livni suggests that one of the reasons she left Mossad was because of the isolating, solitary life it required her to lead. Even her closest family members were not allowed to know she was a spy. When her father visited her in Paris, where she gave the appearance of having no job, he apparently could not understand why his daughter, a brilliant law student, "was wasting her time in Europe doing nothing".

Any long-lasting romance was out of the question because, as Livni put it, "a romantic relationship requires honesty". Furthermore, while she could be proud of her achievements as a member of Bayonet, the elite section of Mossad in which she was highly valued, these too could not be shared with anyone else.

On the other hand, there are certain attractions about leading a double life and the secrecy that it entails. Livni was "loaded with adrenaline" when she was undercover. In these circumstances, every ordinary aspect of daily life becomes highly charged and potentially lethal. It is the secret that must be kept at all costs that gives such intensity to life and that also alienates the person from engaging with life.

This is an exciting mixture—the "secret" life feels more real than any other and can easily become addictive. The double takes over. By entering into a double life of her own, Livni was identifying with her parents. The idea of the double, also known as the *dybbuk* in Jewish folklore and as the *doppelgänger* in German, is a common theme in folklore and fairytales. Dostoyevsky's novel *The Double* vividly describes how an unassuming petty bureaucrat becomes taken over and eventually destroyed by his alter ego, or double, who represents all the repressed and ruthless aspects of his personality.

Otto Rank, one of Freud's first followers, viewed the double as an "energetic denial of the power of death", just as the immortal soul was considered the double for the body. Rank argued that the double protected the ego from extinction. It was a kind of insurance policy against death, creating an illusion of another life that has no limits and no end.

The double appears to be one thing when in fact it is another; there is a secret narrative being played out that no one else is aware of. This is what Freud describes in his essay on *The Uncanny* (1919) in which what is familiar becomes strange and terrifying because it is both familiar and not. Invariably, there is an involuntary repetition of something from the past that is being repeated in the present as if the person is being possessed by another part of himself that is unknown.

Was Livni repeating something from her own past when she was living out this secret life? It turns out that both Livni's parents had been arrested in Israel for terrorist crimes in the 1940s.

Livni's mother had been a member of the militant Zionist group, Irgun, that operated in Palestine during the British mandate. Disguised as pregnant, she robbed a train carrying £35,000 and blew up another en route from Jerusalem to Tel Aviv. Livni's father attacked a British military base and was sentenced to fifteen years in jail and escaped.

In her involvement with Mossad, it is clear that Livni was following in her parents' patriotic footsteps. It is also clear that she had grown up in a family whose members were used to keeping deadly secrets and conducting double lives.

As a young girl growing up in this environment, it is not surprising that Livni might have a natural attraction to becoming a spy and that she would be used to living with family secrets that she could not know about.

By entering into a double life of her own, Livni was not only identifying with her parents, but she was reconstructing an atmosphere of secrecy and danger that may well have pervaded family life, at least subconsciously. As it turned out, this was a life that she recognised she could not continue, or continue to repeat, as the price was too high.

16 February 2009

11

Why Josef Fritzl thought rape was a "lovely idea"

By keeping his daughter in a dungeon, Fritzl was exercising the control denied to him by his mother

"Light out. Rape. Light on. Mould. Rape. In front of the children. The Uncertainty. Birth. Death. Rape." This is the mantra that kept Elisabeth Fritzl sane for twenty-four years locked up in her father's cellar.

Above ground, everything seemed normal. Below ground, it was a horror story. At the opening of Josef Fritzl's trial this week, Christiane Burkheiser, the state prosecutor, passed around a shoebox to the jury containing objects taken from the cellar. Whatever was in the shoebox, the jurors reacted with disgust.

There is a curious symmetry about Josef Fritzl's two families. Fritzl lived upstairs with his wife, Rosemarie, where they had raised seven children and subsequently adopted three grandchildren. Meanwhile, unbeknownst to his family upstairs, Fritzl also lived downstairs in the cellar with his daughter, Elisabeth, where she gave birth to seven children after being raped continuously by her father.

The two families seem to represent two parts of Fritzl's personality: the public face of the family man described as affectionate with his grandchildren and honest and polite at work; and the perverse face of the man in the cellar who was "addicted" to sex with his daughter, and kept her and three of their seven children captive in horrific conditions with no warm water, fresh air, or daylight for twenty-four years.

Fritzl has been assessed as having a "profound personality disorder". His lawyer, Rudolf Mayer, urged the jury "to keep emotion out of this". On the other hand, Mayer attempted to portray his client as having normal feelings of care and concern for his cellar family. Mayer argued that "a man who put so much effort into keeping two families cannot be called a monster. If I only want a daughter as a sex slave, I don't let her bring children into the world. You'd let them starve."

He has emphasised that Fritzl "felt remorse for his personality and what it did to his victims". The implication is that it was Fritzl's "personality" that harmed his victims, not Fritzl himself. And perhaps there is some truth to this, as it emerged that Fritzl's cellar life may well have been the enactment of a perverse fantasy life that Fritzl had to keep locked up inside him and that he dared not expose to the light of day.

Fritzl's story, according to Mayer, is that he had a miserable childhood brought up by a mother who made it clear that she had not wanted him, and a virtually absent father. Fritzl's mother forbade him to have friends and beat him until the age of twelve when, apparently, Fritzl threatened to beat her back.

He is depicted as a captive of his mother, locked in her world, with no father to intervene or protect him against her assaults. The similarity of Fritzl's cellar world is obvious, although the shoe is on the other foot. In Fritzl's cellar, he was the one in control. Fritzl admitted to Mayer: "The cellar in my building belonged to me and me alone—it was my kingdom, that only I had access to."

In his cellar world, Fritzl was not only in complete control, but he could wreak revenge on the mother who imprisoned him in his childhood by his repeated attacks against his daughter, to which he also admits he was addicted.

He could play the part of the mother who tortured and emotionally raped her child, and he could also become, in his fantasy, his mother's partner and have babies with her, triumphing over his need for a father.

Fritzl claims that his sexual relations with his daughter were consensual, despite her testimony that she was chained to a wall. The act of raping his daughter was addictive not only in the omnipotent excitement it gave Fritzl, but it also provided a way for him to discharge his hatred towards his mother while at the same time keeping the relationship alive. Better a hateful relationship than no relationship at all. Fritzl had constructed a fantasy life that in many respects replicated his childhood but was also a denial and a triumph over the reality of his childhood.

Just as in his past, there had been no father to protect him from his mother's hatred, in the cellar there was no metaphorical father, no super-ego within Fritzl to protect him or his daughter and children from their imprisonment in a world of hate.

As long as Fritzl could perpetuate the sado-masochistic world of his childhood in the cellar, he was safe from having to face the grim reality of a hateful mother and an indifferent father—a reality that might have tipped him over into psychosis.

Fritzl allegedly thought it was a "lovely idea" to have a family in the cellar. And for Fritzl, it was just this—by keeping his fantasy family in the cellar, he could keep his madness locked up and safely contained in the confines of his unconscious. His remorse and his concern are most probably genuine for what happened to his daughter and the children he sired with her (including one baby who died after he refused to call for medical help).

At the same time, he needed to use his daughter in creating this fantasy world so as not to go completely mad. At an unconscious level, it seems that the rest of the family upstairs may have been complicit in keeping Fritzl's madness below ground in their denial of what was going on.

Rosemarie, Fritzl's wife, does not seem to have questioned either her daughter's disappearance, falsely explained by her running off to join an extremist sect, or the appearance of grandchildren that suddenly turned up for adoption.

Fritzl's criminal behaviour has a history. He had been convicted of raping a woman in Linz in 1967 and served a term in prison for this. This seems to indicate that he had little control over his impulses, and he may well have been anxious that this could happen again.

"Around 1981 or 1982", as Fritzl admitted, he started preparing his cellar for its first occupant. In 1984, Elisabeth disappeared. At his trial, after his face emerged from hiding behind that blue folder, Fritzl remained expressionless to the public except for an occasional smile—perhaps at his own triumph in achieving twenty-four years of outwitting reality.

18 March 2009

12
How Jade Goody became the new Princess Diana

The victimhood and very public deaths of Jade Goody and the People's Princess have much in common

Jade Goody and Princess Diana had much in common, not least the psychological roots of their stratospheric popularity. Like Jade, Diana was portrayed as a victim of the press, right up to the ravening presence of the paparazzi at her moment of death. Like Jade, Diana portrayed herself as a victim, in Diana's case of the royal family.

The story line is archetypal: the heroine sins, repents by claiming she was a victim of her circumstances, and attains love through her suffering. It is the universal story of the innocent woman who has been tainted by external forces and redeems herself through sacrifice—ultimately through death. She is the willing scapegoat, or in Goody's words, "escape goat", who sacrifices herself to purify the sins of others and to maintain the established order. This is the masochist's revenge against a world that has caused her harm.

This is something that that master of popular psychology, Max Clifford, had acutely realised. Under his tutelage, Jade managed to transform herself from a figure of scandal and ridicule to an icon of heroic suffering. Clifford told us how Jade came to him for help when her career was at rock bottom: "I knew her well enough to know that she was more sinned against than sinning."

It's a remark that perhaps summed up Jade Goody's appeal to the public more than anything else—being sinned against has been her greatest trump card. And her unsuccessful battle against cancer dramatically epitomised Goody's fight between the forces of good and evil.

We can see a turning point in Jade's career in her interview with *News of the World* following her racist attack on Shilpa Shetty on *Big Brother*. Jade sobs on camera, apologising for her bullying and claiming ignorance of what she was doing. She says: "I don't want anybody to feel they're scared of me or intimidated by me. I just don't know how to argue ... I've been brought up on watching people argue and swear ... It was what I'd ... the aggression that I held. And I don't want that aggression and I will make sure I get help so that aggression doesn't come out again."

The apology was heartfelt, but what comes across most pointedly is her statement that she was "brought up on watching people argue and swear"—the implication being that this is all she knew. Thus does the sinner become the sinned against. The ray of hope is that Goody also acknowledges that she needs help in controlling her aggression.

Here, Goody had a chance of taking charge of her life and not continuing to be life's victim. But this would mean resisting the attraction of capitalising on her victim status and breaking the masochistic cycle.

Goody's iconic yet ambivalent status is vividly portrayed in a mural, possibly the work of the artist Banksy, that has appeared recently in Kentish Town, north London: in it, she is depicted as bald, with a pound sign branded on her forehead and vultures circling above her head.

The message is clear: Goody has become the victim of our modern world of celebrity greed, branding, and media exploitation. And while this may be true, there is the question of how complicit, how willing, she was to revel in her own mortification—as Diana did. By transforming herself into a heroic victim, Goody appealed to both men and women in a powerful way, much as Diana did. Women can identify with the masochistic victim who has suffered at the hands of others, whose anger and aggression is attributed to a reaction to maltreatment, and who is essentially blameless.

Women in this role are idealised—the greater their suffering, the greater their cause—and at the same time they are stripped of agency. They remain victims of a sadistic world—in Goody's case, the parents who "argue and swear". They appeal for mercy. And all along, their continued suffering is a passive attack on the bad parents, as if to say, "look at what you have turned me into". This is not just an attack but also a bid for love—"you will love me more if I suffer and allow you to abuse me".

For women who have seen themselves as relatively powerless in society, this masochistic self-image offers a perverse illusion of power—the power of being a victim. For men, this is an image of woman that is compelling—it makes them feel that they are in some way responsible for alleviating the woman's suffering and confers an illusion of power on them as protectors and, unconsciously, as sadists.

The net effect is that this scenario restores the image of women as helpless and men as powerful—an age-old story that satisfies something in everyone. And one of which Jade and Diana are archetypal protagonists.

22 March 2009

13

Nicholas Hughes was killed by Sylvia Plath, his envious mother

Tortured by the ghost of his envious mother, Nicholas Hughes's suicide was inevitable

Nicholas Hughes had a nightmare start in life. His mother, Sylvia Plath, had a history of fighting her own inner demons that must have made it especially difficult for her to be there in her mind for her two children, Frieda and Nicholas—born a year apart.

Her husband, Ted Hughes, separated from Sylvia before Nicholas's first birthday, and only months later Sylvia committed suicide. As a small infant, Nicholas would have been extremely sensitive to his mother's depression, and this would leave an indelible fault line in his own personality. Forty-six years after his mother committed suicide, Nicholas has followed suit by hanging himself at his home in Alaska.

Children whose parents have committed suicide—at no matter what age—tend to feel not only responsible for their parents' depression and ultimate suicide, but also profoundly rejected by them.

In short, the parent who kills herself is perceived by the child as not loving him enough to want to live. Any close relationships that might arise subsequently are fraught with trauma, insecurity, and dread.

The impotence experienced by the child in not being able to keep his parent alive is also unbearable. If the child is very young, as Nicholas was, it may leave him feeling that his love is lethal and can only result in death and loss. The experience of loving is tainted from the start.

Nicholas Hughes did not marry and had no children. We might speculate that this felt too risky and dangerous an undertaking for him. Nevertheless, he is mourned by family and friends as "an adventurous marine biologist with a distinguished academic career behind him and a host of friends and achievements in his own right".

What is most striking about the timing of his suicide is that it seems to have coincided with his resigning from his university post and setting up a pottery at home. A family friend explained that Nicholas wanted to devote time "to advance his not inconsiderable talent at making pots and creatures in clay". It is possible that this decision was the tipping point in his life.

Although Nicholas struggled with depression for much of his life, he does not seem to have inherited Plath's manic depression, instead suffering from his own psychological conflicts relating to the circumstances of his life.

However, there may be an important clue to the timing of his suicide in a poem that Sylvia Plath wrote about him shortly before her own suicide. In "Nick and the Candlestick", published in her collection *Ariel*, Plath writes, "You are the one/Solid the spaces lean on, envious./You are the baby in the barn." These are haunting lines that convey how precious this baby was to Plath, but at the same time there is an envy of him, of the solidity that she sees in him, that she leans on and does not possess herself.

To Plath, this small child, who may have seemed self-contained and intact, reinforced her own sense of damage and emptiness, along with her inevitable anxieties about being able to give enough to him when she was embroiled in what Hughes was later to describe as the "hidden workshop of herself".

The prospect for Nicholas of making his own babies ("clay creatures") in the barn may have been overwhelming for a number of reasons. On one level, he may have been aware, unconsciously, that he was embarking on something that he felt would have made his mother painfully envious of him—of the solidity in him that she felt she did not have—the solidity that would have made it possible for him to be creative despite his traumatic beginnings.

At the same time, his desire to express his emotional life creatively in his pottery may have triggered off a deeper awareness of the dreadful and frightening emptiness he most likely would have experienced as an infant with a depressed and self-occupied mother—a mother who would have struggled to hold him in her mind emotionally and who then deserted him in death.

The loneliness, vulnerability, and rage that is left by such an experience can be intolerable when it resurfaces. To overcome this and to find a way of living and of being creative can feel like a monumental task, especially in the face of an envious ghost who had not been able to achieve this herself.

In the end, it seems that Nicholas's identification with his mother and the pain of losing her was too powerful to survive. Hughes's poem, following Plath's death, described how his son's eyes "Became wet jewels,/The hardest substance of the purest pain/As I fed him in his high white chair."

23 March 2009

14
Inside this head: how paranoia turned Phil Spector into a killer

The term "paranoia" originates from the Greek meaning madness or disorder of the mind. It is a chronic psychosis that is characterised by systems of delusion that nevertheless leave the intellect functioning. Most typically, the paranoid personality suffers from delusions of persecution. Throughout Phil Spector's arrest and subsequent trials for murder, he has insisted on his innocence, claiming that Lana Clarkson committed suicide because her career was at rock bottom.

Spector then went a step further, expressing his fury that Clarkson had done this *to him*. A transcript of Spector's statement at the time of his arrest records him describing Clarkson as "a piece of shit. And I don't know what her fucking problem was, but she certainly had no right to come to my fucking castle, blow her fucking head and (indecipherable) a murder." During his trial, Spector was shown photographs of Clarkson's blasted head and looked off into the distance, absorbed in himself, without showing any feeling.

The prosecutor in Phil Spector's retrial described him as a "very dangerous man who had a history of playing Russian roulette with women". Five women who had dated Spector—going back to the

1970s—testified that he had pulled weapons on them when they had refused his advances. Ronnie Spector, Phil's first wife until 1972, claimed that he threatened to kill her if she ever left him. John Lennon and Leonard Cohen, both produced by Spector, also had guns drawn on them.

Apparently obsessed with guns, Spector used them to get his way and to establish ultimate power over others. Several weeks before the actress Lana Clarkson's murder in 2003, Spector described himself in an interview as "relatively insane" with a history of emotional turmoil and a bipolar disorder. While his career soared in the music industry, Spector was well known as a bully, provoking his business partners to leave him. For the last twenty-five years, since Spector was injured badly in a car crash, he has been a recluse in his mansion in Alhambra, an unprepossessing suburb of LA. Over this time, Spector has become increasingly frail. In court, he has been described as looking like a crumpled "ventriloquist's dummy". There is also some evidence to suggest that he may have become increasingly paranoid.

Signs of Spector's paranoia became most evident during the course of his first trial when, vehemently defending his innocence, he suggested to friends that the case itself was the culminating chapter of a conspiracy against him going back to the 1960s. Spector imagined that he had been targeted for attack as an icon of counter-culture and a friend of John Lennon. He also likened himself to Dalton Trumbo, a screenwriter abandoned by his friends during the McCarthy hearings, and to Albert Einstein, who had to flee Nazi Germany as a suspected Jew.

Of course, if anyone threatens a lot of people with guns, they are most likely—even justified—in having paranoid fantasies. However, it is also possible that Spector's fascination with guns and his bullying behaviour were by-products of a paranoid part of his personality. Spector's father had committed suicide when he was nine years old. This would most certainly have traumatised Spector and made him feel extremely anxious about his masculine identification with his father as well as his feelings towards other men. His seemingly constant need to compel women to have sexual relations with him—with his gun—and not to leave him suggests a highly insecure masculine identity and may mask homosexual feelings that Spector was never able to reconcile within himself.

In his mind, Spector is the man who is plotted against and hated due to other people's envy of his phallic abilities. He is the one with the gun that can decide life or death. This is not only a possible reversal of Spector's impotence in the face of his father's suicide, but it may also be an identification or remnant of the father he idealised and wished to be like yet who failed him in death. Spector's inevitable anger with his father for killing himself could also contribute to his paranoid feelings. Spector's insistence that Clarkson killed herself and his rage at her for doing so may also in some way be his bid for the sympathy that he never received as a child.

The irony is that, if Spector had pleaded "relatively insane", he might well have received a softer sentence in a psychiatric institution that would have also been considerably shorter than the prison sentence he is now likely to face.

15 April 2009

15

Why *Britain's Got Talent*'s Susan Boyle makes people weep

Unassuming yet quietly confident, the astonishing rise by the Scottish singing spinster is a tale of two egos

Several patients—both women and men—have told me about the moving success story of [*Britain's Got Talent* singer] Susan Boyle with tears pouring down their cheeks. As one patient put it: "I've spent most of my life trying to be so good, to do the right thing, to be perfect and it's been such a waste of time, a waste of life. Susan Boyle has broken through all that stuff and has gone ahead and done what she's wanted to do. She doesn't have to be somebody she's not."

Max Clifford, the publicist, points out that the "magical moments which we as a nation love" are those that challenge our assumptions and prejudices. Boyle has challenged the stereotype of what it takes to be a successful woman—Cinderella has not been transformed into a Princess, she has been a Princess all along, but without the material trappings of one.

"*I dreamed a dream in time gone by, when hope was high and life worth living.*" These are the opening—and extraordinarily apt—lyrics of Susan Boyle's astonishing and unexpected rave performance last week on *Britain's Got Talent*. A dumpy, forty-seven-year-old single Scottish woman, Boyle is the epitome of the old maid who has long gone past her sell-by date. She lives alone with her cat, Pebbles, openly professes that she has *never* been kissed, is unemployed, and has spent most of her adult life doing charitable work and, more recently, caring for her mother, who died in 2007.

The youngest of nine children, Boyle developed learning difficulties as a result of being deprived of oxygen at her birth. She was bullied throughout her childhood by other children, although very much protected within her family. Music had always been important in the family, and Boyle grew up singing and never stopped.

She has sung in small theatrical productions, in the church choir, and is well known on the local karaoke circuit. But she was going nowhere with her career. Her mother had first suggested that she should audition for *Britain's Got Talent* following the success of Paul Potts, and it was perhaps her mother's belief in her that played an important part in helping Boyle's dream come true.

Boyle made it clear when she first appeared on stage that "I've always wanted to perform in front of a large audience." She was sassy and uninhibited, while at the same time maintaining her professional cool. She was doing something she had always wanted to do, and she was giving it her best. After her success, she said she felt "quietly confident", and when asked about her future, said emphatically that these were "baby steps" and it was just the beginning. Boyle remains modest and realistic, commenting on the mistakes she made in her performance from which she needs to learn.

In psychoanalytic terms, Boyle's performance highlights the difference between the ego-ideal and the superego. The Austrian psychoanalyst Annie Reich explains, "The ego-ideal represents what one wishes to be, the superego what one ought to be."

The ego-ideal is initially based on an idealised image of the parents that the child internalises and that is gradually modified as the child grows and incorporates other characteristics from his environment that form a model to aspire to. In healthy development, the superego tempers these aspirations by reminding the ego of its limitations—it keeps the ego grounded.

When there is a disturbance in the child's early relationships and the child does not have a good sense of himself and of being loved, this can impair the development of a strong ego, and the child may become susceptible to a megalomaniac ego-ideal along with a demanding and punitive superego.

The child attributes the fact that he is not loved to his failure to fulfil the parents' wishes of who they want him to be. These are the conditions in which an ego-ideal is imposed from without. The child does not aspire to an image that is a mixture of his good feelings about himself and his idealisation of his parents; instead, the child identifies with and strives for an image of who he ought to be because he feels he has in some way failed to obtain his parents' love. Inevitably, this is an image of perfection that is unattainable, and the harsh superego will settle for nothing less.

The cult of the celebrity is today's primary example of an ego-ideal imposed from without, and it has an utterly crippling effect on ordinary development. What is so moving about Boyle's trajectory of success is that she demonstrates the victory of the ego-ideal that is genuinely based on "what one wishes to be" as opposed to an imposed ideal from the outside that is predicated on "what one ought to be".

There is a difference between wanting to perform in front of a large audience and wanting to be a celebrity. Boyle's success is not that she has been a victim who has vanquished her enemies, but that she has the courage to be herself. We cry because we see in her the seeds of our own liberation.

20 April 2009

16
Torturing terrorists is bad for your health

The pain suffered by individuals and states when they use "enhanced interrogation techniques"

A patient of mine, in a fit of rage, cried out, "Two can play at this game. I'm going to torture my brother just like he has tortured me all these years. I've been terrified of him and if I don't fight back, he'll wipe me out. It's the only way to stop him!" There was a depressed silence and he then said, "The only thing that stops me is that I know if I did this, he would just hit back even harder. It wouldn't stop him—in fact, it's exactly what he wants me to do so the game will go on forever—we'll forever be locked in battle. It's like a terminal bond. And at the end of the day, I would hate myself even more than I hate him. I'd be no different than him. He'd really win then."

What my patient said encapsulates much of the dynamics of the torturer and the tortured. My patient has for many years been terrorised by a psychopathic brother who has been intent on destroying him. He has felt helpless, frightened, and trapped. He has also felt murderous.

My patient's initial impulse to hit back echoes Dick Cheney's statement only two months ago: "These are evil people. And we're not going to win this fight by turning the other cheek ... If it hadn't been for what we did with respect to the ... enhanced interrogation techniques for high-value detainees … then we would have been attacked again."

Whether or not there is evidence for this, the battle with the terrorist factions of al-Qaeda in the West goes on with the threat of further reprisals and an escalation of violence.

It has now become clear by the findings of the Red Cross that torture was committed under the banner of "enhanced interrogation techniques". More and more gruelling evidence is emerging of the scarring and traumatic effects of torture on its victims.

Far less is said about its effects on the perpetrators and those in the line of command. What emerges in many of the trials of those responsible for torture, such as the current Khmer Rouge trial in Cambodia, is an extreme level of fear that is at the root of torture. In his recent testimony, Comrade Duch, who served under Pol Pot's regime, explained: "When I was forced to supervise (the prison), I became both an actor in criminal acts and a hostage of the regime." If he did not follow orders, his own life would have been at stake.

Within the US, the fear generated by the terrorist attacks of 2001 has been overwhelming and has led to an intense paranoid response, as expressed most dramatically in Bush's declaration of a "War on Terror". The once invincible nation, never before invaded, has suddenly been made to feel vulnerable and helpless in the face of an enemy from without that attacks without warning and under cover.

This has given credence to the myth of the "ticking bomb" that has influenced so much of US policy in responding to terrorism. In this scenario, there is a bomb waiting to go off and a prisoner who knows—or whom we imagine knows—the whereabouts of the bomb. The damage caused by the bomb could be immense and terrifying. The torture of the prisoner is justified because it elicits the whereabouts of the bomb and allows it to be detonated harmlessly. The torturer—and those who order torture—are affirmed in their role of saviour. Justice and revenge and cultural cleansing are served at the same time. Does this begin to sound like the ideology of the enemy?

Especially when the enemy is from without, it is very easy to personify them as "other". They embody everything that is bad and dangerous that we would like to deny in ourselves. The good guys and the bad guys are split into two clear camps. By projecting all the evil onto "these people", we not only remain pure but the tactics we use to exterminate evil are exonerated.

In our self-justifications we become virtually identical to the extremist religious terrorists who similarly believe they are ridding the world of evil. We are copying them, and in doing so we become like them. Even the techniques of torture adopted by the US are based on techniques used by our "enemies", notably those used by the Chinese Communists in the Korean War and those used by the Soviet intelligence services.

Torture is justified along these lines and because it works. It has been used as a tool in combating terrorism/enemy action throughout the centuries. In the recent US incidents of torture, it is also justified, ironically, as a means of protecting US citizens from being targeted by terrorists as objects of hatred. Terrorism is so frightening precisely because it treats the individual as an object.

The ultimate aim of terrorism is to destroy the "other" by stripping them of their humanity. And it is our humanity that must be protected—at all costs. What is increasingly apparent from the evidence coming out of Guantanamo Bay and other sites is the dehumanisation of the victims who are tortured. This is what is also at the heart of terrorism.

The torturer not only wants to force the enemy to disclose the whereabouts of the ticking bomb, but, like my patient, the torturer wants revenge for the anxiety and torture he (or his country) have been put through. In the act of torture, the torturer turns the tables. He becomes omnipotent in his fantasy and wants to make his victim feel helpless, trapped, and terrified so that he can be rid of these feelings inside himself. He expels his terror into the terrorist, the "other", who is further dehumanised.

It is not possible to conduct torture of any kind without dehumanising the victim. However, this also requires the torturer to become dehumanised, and here is the rub. In order to do his job, the torturer must cut off from his feelings of concern and empathy towards the other and turn the victim into an object, not a person. This also explains why the job of torturer at times attracts people who already suffer from such a split in their psyches.

However, for those who are more intact emotionally, the act of committing torture necessitates a perversion of their emotions. It becomes very difficult, if not impossible, for the torturer to allow himself to feel true compassion without opening the floodgates of guilt, remorse, and horror. The torturer is condemned to a twilight of numbed experience in which his feelings need to be suppressed so that he can continue to function. There is a striking parallel with the massive denial that victims of torture need to put into place in order to survive their ordeals. Torturer and tortured become dehumanised images of one another.

The real dilemma about condoning torture—and now about whether the torturers should be pardoned or not—is perhaps less about human rights or issues of legality but more about the fact that what was an enemy from without becomes an enemy from within when the collective psyche becomes corrupted by this process of dehumanisation. This is perhaps the greatest danger of allowing torture to continue. It is simply bad psychology.

22 April 2009

17
The psychological trauma behind surrogate pregnancies

**Why Sarah Jessica Parker and Matthew Broderick
opted for a surrogate pregnancy**

Life imitates fiction. What is more appropriate than Sarah Jessica
Parker, star of *Sex and the City*, having twins via a surrogate mother
with her actor husband, Matthew Broderick?

The women in *Sex and the City* want all the things that men
want—and more. They want to be rich and powerful, free in their
sexual relations, able to have babies and carry on as if nothing has
happened, and believe that anything is possible if there is enough
money to pay for it.

The reality is that it doesn't work like that. Even with surrogate
motherhood, an increasingly popular solution to infertility or the
incapacity to have a baby, there are psychological hazards beneath
the surface.

While Sarah Jessica Parker and Matthew Broderick, who
already have a six-year-old son but have been unable to conceive
since, are not imitations of the characters in *Sex and the City*, their
announcement that they have employed a surrogate mother, due
to give birth this summer, raises questions not only about morality
but about the psychology of prospective parents who choose this
option. The baby represents a magical phallus that can be created
at will without effort.

Surrogate motherhood appeals to many women—and men—for different reasons. In the case of Sarah Jessica Parker and Matthew Broderick, they have made it clear that they were "desperate" for another child of their own.

This is perhaps the most frequently cited reason and, apart from the fact that the reality favours the rich over the poor, it signifies that there may be increasing difficulty in accepting our human limitations and consequent losses. Age and physical incapacity can be magicked away when someone else can have your baby for you.

A New York writer, Alex Kuczynski, who chose surrogate motherhood, sums up her experience. "As the months passed, something curious happened: The bigger Cathy was, the more I realised that I was glad—practically euphoric—I was not pregnant. I was in a daze of anticipation, but I was also secretly, curiously, perpetually relieved, unburdened from the sheer physicality of pregnancy ... Cathy was getting bigger and the constraints on her grew. I, on the other hand, was happy to exploit my last few months of non-motherhood by white-water rafting down Level 10 rapids on the Colorado River, racing down a mountain at sixty miles per hour at ski-racing camp, drinking bourbon, and going to the Super Bowl."

In short, surrogate motherhood is also a great solution if you are a woman and want to go on doing all the things that men do without the "physicality" of being a woman with a woman's body.

The most worrying aspect psychologically of surrogate motherhood is that it bypasses the actual creative process of bearing children. A baby becomes something that is manufactured elsewhere, vicariously, without the physical and emotional processes that naturally occur during pregnancy and childbirth.

The actual work of making a baby is farmed out to someone else, and this necessarily turns the process into artifice. At its most extreme, the product, the baby, represents a magical phallus that can be created at will without effort or experience. In this respect, the baby becomes in fantasy a substitute for the real thing and confers omnipotence to the person possessing it.

Surrogate motherhood opens the door for the possibility of anyone being able to produce a baby—as long as they can pay for it. The problem is that it is a fake—just like going to the bakery and buying a cake and passing it off as one's own.

This deception comes about when there is overwhelming internal pressure on the ego to conform to some ideal that is beyond its means. The pressure to create a "fake" baby may also indicate that the mother and/or the father suffer from a deep sense of rejection—an early narcissistic wound—that makes any inadequacy or limitation unbearable to acknowledge.

The parents who produce a child through surrogacy can maintain an unconscious one-upmanship over parents who produce children normally. Through their special powers, they can fill in the gap in their lives that has made them feel inadequate, and they can avoid having to acknowledge their envy of parents who can make their own babies. The tables are turned, and they become the envied rather than the other way around.

Unfortunately, like in *Sex and the City*, this narcissistic attempt to make up for what is lost throws up serious difficulties in reality. The pressure to maintain this degree of omnipotence and to avoid pain and loss is likely to take its toll on the entire family.

In addition to this, there is substantial evidence that babies are highly attuned to their mothers' bodies (that is, taste, smell, touch, sound) *in utero*. We do not yet know the full impact on the baby of the loss of its mother at birth, except that it undoubtedly exacerbates an experience that is already traumatic. The failure to recognise the importance of pre-natal attachment suggests a desire to minimise the importance of attachment, separation, and loss for the baby. Surrogacy may be at the cost of these basic needs in the case of the baby as well as the parents, much less the surrogate mother.

6 May 2009

18

Farrah Fawcett in denial as she films cancer battle

There can be no happy ending to *Farrah's Story*, despite the Charlie's Angel actress's attempts to transform her death by documenting her suffering

Ryan O'Neal turns to Farrah Fawcett, lying emaciated on her death bed, and says, "We did very well last night." She says, "What were the numbers?" They are not talking about a re-make of *Love Story*, this is *Farrah's Story*, the ninety-minute documentary aired on NBC last week of Fawcett's fight against cancer—a fight she is losing rapidly. Fawcett's showbiz joke about ratings has a double edge in this case as it is undoubtedly her final performance. And the on-again/off-again love affair between O'Neal and Fawcett has never been stronger.

Fawcett, now aged sixty-two, discovered she had cancer of the bowel in 2006 and has been fighting ever since. After chemotherapy failed, she was told by her doctors that she would have to undergo major surgery and that she would be required to wear a permanent colostomy bag. Instead of following her doctors' advice, Fawcett turned to two German specialists who offered her a "less drastic" treatment called chemoembolisation—chemicals injected directly into the affected organs—at a cost of £3,500 a session. After a cocktail of further vitamins and chemical treatment, Fawcett was assured she was cured, and the doctors claimed it was "a miracle".

The truth was painfully revealed a few weeks later when Fawcett's scan showed that the cancer had spread to her liver.

The documentary, filmed and narrated by Fawcett's best friend, Alana Stewart (Rod Stewart's ex-wife), was intended to show Fawcett's victory over the disease and to be an inspiration to others. Tragically, as the story unfolds, we hear Fawcett sobbing, "I thought I would be cured". Although this would seem like an admission of failure, Fawcett, Stewart, and O'Neal nevertheless continue to hope for a miracle even when the odds are clearly against it.

Fawcett's indomitable fight against cancer is not only a desire to overcome the odds and to strive to live, it also stems from a fear of dying that is so overwhelming that reality itself needs to be constantly kept at bay. Fawcett's fear certainly fuelled her search for a cure but also made her particularly susceptible to exploitation and false promises. The documentary portrays the tremendous pressure among all those involved to collude with Fawcett in denying the inevitable. This pressure is all too familiar to those who are close to someone suffering from a terminal illness and poses enormous conflicts both ethically and emotionally.

The difficulty about denial in these circumstances, and the pressure to sustain it, is that it robs everyone of being able to say goodbye properly and to accept this final separation. David Rieff, in writing about his mother Susan Sontag's fight against cancer, points out that "it was impossible even to tell her—in a deep way, I mean—that I loved her because to have done so would have been to say: 'You're dying'". When reality is denied in this way, feelings are also inevitably suppressed, and the impending loss cannot be thought about, experienced, or shared. Rather than easing the fear of death and loss, paradoxically, it intensifies it for everyone.

The added twist to Fawcett's denial is her attempt to transform her death through making it into a documentary in which she can observe herself playing the role of someone who is dying. In this case, that someone happens to be herself. Life can be fictionalised and the real trauma contained within a filmic narrative that, like in Woody Allen's *Purple Rose of Cairo*, the subject can step in and out of at will. The actual making of the documentary may have been Fawcett's way of dealing with what was unthinkable and unspeakable. Playing to the camera also ensures that there is always an audience to witness the pain and suffering, and perhaps, most importantly, that one is not left alone—for it is the aloneness of death that is most unbearable.

The act of filming death confers a power over life that does not exist in reality. Nine million viewers tuned in to watch *Farrah's Story*. Critics described it as "exploitative", "awful", "unbearable", and "fascinating". The overwhelming attraction to this form of reality television is that it allows us all to have the illusion that we are entering into the most private area of someone else's life—especially someone who, because of the their public status, represents a powerful figure. We become children who are peeking into our parents' bedroom to find out what really goes on.

But the voyeurism surrounding death has a further attraction, much like our fascination—and horror—with watching violence. Because the violence is at a distance and usually depicts someone who is a stranger to us, we can in our fantasy transcend the trauma and reality of what is happening. The act of filming death means that it already confers the filmmaker and viewer a power over life that does not exist in reality.

It is no surprise that delinquent gangs regularly film the violence they commit and circulate it to their peers. They are not only demonstrating how powerful they are, but they are attempting to transform something that is traumatic and destructive into something that is pleasurable and exciting. The real feelings are anaesthetised, and this is the whole point. Denial is not only located in Fawcett's failure to accept that she has lost her battle against cancer, it infects all of us as viewers who want to believe that this could never happen to us.

20 May 2009

19
Why swine flu and torture provoke witch hunts

The witch hunts over American torture practices, swine flu, and terrorism are a backlash against Obama's inclusive policies

Witch hunts come in different guises. While MPs in the UK are being pilloried for their expenses, witch hunting in the US is taking a different form. The recent controversy about whether or not to release yet more photographs of US military personnel depicting abuse of captives in Iraq and Afghanistan serves as an instructive episode for us to study the psychology of the witch hunt.

Reversing his earlier decision to release the detainee photos, Obama justifies his position on the basis that the images could "further inflame anti-American opinion". The anxiety on the part of US Defence Department, voiced by Defence Secretary Robert Gates, is "that the release of these photographs will cost American lives" because they would incite a backlash among extremist groups in the Middle East.

This argument is countered by the American Civil Liberties Union (ACLU) and other human rights groups in the US and abroad, on the grounds that evidence of torture must be made public in order to raise public awareness and to act as a deterrent against further acts of torture. The witches are the ones who are trying to cover up torture.

A closer look at Obama's change of mind suggests that it may in fact be a brave decision that, paradoxically, at a psychological level, protects human rights and interests. While the ACLU is concerned to expose such quasi-criminal behaviour, there is nevertheless a danger of creating scapegoats out of the torturers and thereby failing to address some of the deeper, underlying causes that foster this kind of behaviour.

This is the psychology behind the witch hunt. We want to punish and remove the torturers in order to uproot this evil from our midst. But mixed in with our desire for justice and revenge, there is also a desire to project our sadism into the torturers and in this way to be rid of our own hatred and destructiveness. The Salem witch trials of seventeenth-century New England were virulent attempts to cleanse society of its ills and had a cathartic, albeit temporary, effect by making the persecutors feel self-righteous and pure.

The ACLU asserts that increased awareness of the practice of torture will serve as a deterrent. This argument rests on the assumption that human behaviour can be altered through moral pressure and example. If this were really the case, we would not have the problems we have now.

Although those who order, command, and commit torture are responsible for their actions, they provide a warning sign that there has been a perverse takeover in the psyche of the culture. The warning signs need to be taken seriously. But the idea that torture can be uprooted through vilification is seductive in its simplicity.

Obama's decision points out a hidden danger in this approach. The release of more detainee photographs provides ammunition for a fresh round of reprisals and plays into the spiralling witch-hunt mentality. There is, as Obama argues, already public evidence and responsibility taken for the military abuses that have been committed. The need to disclose every instance of wrongdoing can be seen as a desire for absolution and purification.

However, it may also pave the way for the US to revert to the position that torture is something done by others—by the "foreign witches"—and that it is not an American activity—or not any longer.

The Iraq and Afghanistan extremists may well react out of revenge and may well rise to the provocation that they are the witches, not the Americans. If this happens, the US can then triumph by once again becoming an innocent victim—a victim who has said he's sorry, has atoned for his sins, and is still attacked by his persecutors. It may be an act of self-flagellation that provokes a sadistic response and leaves the US as a martyr of purity.

While the political left continue their rampage for full disclosure of detainee abuses, a fresh attack has been launched by the political right against Obama's intention to close Guantanamo.

Last week, the US Senate rejected Obama's request for funds to shut Guantanamo with a vote of ninety to six. This decision followed the testimony of FBI Director Robert Mueller, who claimed that nearly fourteen per cent of those who have been released from Guantanamo since it opened in 2002 have been involved in subsequent terrorist activities.

On the one hand, Obama is seen as trying to cover up the crimes of the US military, and on the other hand, he is criticised for failing to be tough enough and to protect civilians from the threat of further terrorist attacks. The witch hunt against Obama's policies seems to have infected both political extremes.

Witch hunting can also be spotted in the recent panic surrounding swine flu—another scourge to be exterminated from American soil. Significantly enough, swine flu migrated from Mexico across the border and is regarded within the US with as much fear and hostility (and perhaps hysteria) as that shown towards other migrants, such as the Mexicans themselves.

Terrorists, torture, and swine flu must be contained and eradicated from the culture. Each is regarded as a foreign body that has invaded and contaminated a country that prides itself on the highest levels of emotional and physical hygiene.

It may be no coincidence that the widespread anxiety in the US to expunge a contagious, allegedly deadly disease, to imprison and eradicate terrorists on American soil, and to make transparent all evidence of military abuse so that there is no further contamination, comes in the wake of Obama's assertive policy of global inclusiveness.

Witch hunts invariably stem from an unconscious backlash that strives to preserve the hegemony of the past and to protect the culture from being invaded by what is perceived to be new and foreign.

Obama's attempts to encompass and engage with differences on all levels, on both foreign and domestic fronts, may be more of a threat to the American unconscious than his countrymen wish to recognise.

22 May 2009

20
Ireland needs courage to change cycle of abuse

The child abuse inquiry has shown the Catholic Church must face up to its long history of paedophilia

Vilified for saying it takes "courage" for Irish Catholic clergy involved in child abuse to "face the facts from their past", the new Archbishop of Westminster, the Most Reverend Vincent Nichols, may have unwittingly put his finger on the heart of the problem.

Courage to face the facts seems to have been particularly lacking in the institutions in which abuse remained unchecked and in the deals made throughout the institutional network to protect clergy guilty of abuse. The Christian Brothers, responsible for running the largest number of institutions, only agreed to cooperate in the investigation and to give evidence before the Ryan inquiry in exchange for anonymity of the accused clerics.

People from more than two hundred and fifty church-run institutions gave evidence. Out of these, Judge Sean Ryan, who chaired the inquiry that began nine years ago, praised one order, the Rosminians, for their attempt to understand the abuses that had occurred. Courage may well be what is needed, but it does seem to be in short supply.

The Ryan commission has uncovered a history of widespread child abuse within the industrial schools, orphanages, reformatories, and hostels caring for children in Ireland from the 1930s until their closure in the 1990s, following the election of Mary Robinson as President and emerging concern over the treatment of children throughout the care system.

The abuses against children were often tacitly acknowledged within local communities. In her novel *In the Forest*, Edna O'Brian's central character is a young boy who has gone from one harsh institution to the next, beaten and sexually abused by the priests and boys alike, with the implication that he has become criminally insane as a result.

The extent and severity of the abuse that has been discovered in so many of these institutions has shocked everyone. The girls seemed to have been primarily subjected to beatings and emotional humiliations that undermined their self-esteem. The boys were subject to sexual abuse and paedophilia by priests who were meant to care for them.

These children were vulnerable and impotent, without any protective adult they could turn to. If they ran away from their institution—an option that was usually unsuccessful—they incurred even greater punishment when they were caught and brought back.

There was one way they could retaliate—by becoming passive victims while at the same time identifying with their abusers. Some boys who were bullied and abused tried to gain an illusion of control over their world by themselves becoming bullies and abusers of the boys who were younger and weaker than themselves. This is a good example of the way in which a culture of institutional corruption spreads and is perpetuated. It is something that happens throughout most penal systems—as well as some of Britain's public schools.

Another familiar technique for survival is well known as the Stockholm syndrome, named after an incident in Sweden in 1973 in which the hostages of a bank robbery became emotionally attached to their captors to the point of defending them after they were released from their six-day ordeal.

In such a situation, a sado-masochistic bond is formed in which the victim derives what is perceived to be love from the sadistic treatment of his perpetrator. The victim's masochism enables him to feel powerful in his complete subjugation of himself to an all-powerful entity. No individual will exists, no basic needs exist, and pain is transcended through self-loathing and identification with the aggressor. The victim seeks fusion with the omnipotent sadist and colludes unconsciously with the attack as an act of contempt for his weakness and impotence.

Victims suffer enormous shame when their abuse is disclosed because of their unconscious guilt. The sadist, on the other hand, even as he attacks the weakness and vulnerability of the victim, he is also attacking these characteristics in himself, as represented by the victim. The two form a kind of *folie à deux* in which a hateful attachment is confused with love.

This perverse dynamic becomes even more complex and powerful in the case of paedophilia. The paedophile is compelled to choose a child as a sexual partner because he identifies profoundly with the child—his sexual behaviour is both an attack on the vulnerability of the child that makes the paedophile feel powerful and it is an attempt to love and comfort the child who is at the same time hated.

The paedophile has often been the victim of sexual abuse himself and has failed to develop psychologically and sexually beyond the point of pre-adolescence. The compulsive behaviour of the paedophile is perhaps so deeply abhorred by society because it represents a madness that confuses love and hate, leaving an indelible mark on the child that will taint him for life.

Institutions become corrupt and perverse from the top down. They need a good leader to serve as a father who protects boundaries, sets limits, and acknowledges the power adults have over children and how this power can be abused. These parameters establish a safe framework within which institutional life can function properly. A leader who has not experienced a protective father in his own development will be considerably handicapped in performing this role. He may well turn a blind eye to corruption within the institution or, worse yet, he may become complicit in cultivating it.

The tragic history of so many of the institutions under scrutiny in Ireland reflects more than anything else the degree to which the priests and nuns running them had been irreparably damaged from their own emotional abuse. As the Archbishop of Westminster so rightly said, courage is needed to be able to accept responsibility for the abuses that some of the clergy have committed. He might also have added that courage is needed by many of those concerned to face their own histories as victims of abuse.

26 May 2009

21

Why Americans can't handle John Ensign's affair

America demands strong father figures because of its pioneer history. But John Ensign has lost the trust of his conservative right "children"

When Bill Clinton's affair with Monica Lewinksy was exposed in public, John Ensign, the Nevada Republican, now a possible contender for the next presidential race, declared it "an embarrassing moment for the country". He also went on to say about Clinton: "He has no credibility left."

Now it is Senator Ensign's turn to bring embarrassment on himself and his party with his admission yesterday of his infidelity with a former staff member, known to be Cynthia Hampton.

Much is being made of Ensign's hypocrisy: he is a member of an evangelical church promoting fidelity, he has spoken out about the illicit sexual behaviour of other politicians, and he represents the conservative right of the Republican Party that upholds the values of the family and heterosexuality as central to its political platform.

However, many politicians have weathered accusations of hypocrisy with negligible damage. What is important here is his sexual track record. While in England, and in most of Europe, politicians' affairs generally only raise eyebrows, curiosity, and at times envy, in the US such behaviour is a deal-breaker at the best of times. If a US politician is unfaithful to his wife, there is an implicit assumption that this means he is unfaithful to the American public.

The Puritan heritage is certainly alive and well in the US, but begs the question as to why sexual infidelity should still be such a damnable offence—so much so that it destroys politicians' careers. What springs to mind immediately is Freud's *Totem and Taboo*, written in 1913.

The taboo, according to Freud, has a psychological and cultural purpose in protecting the father within the primal horde from attack. Following on from this, the taboo ensures that the social structure remains intact and is not reduced to a lawless society governed by men's desires, the id, which would result in destructive chaos.

American history, recent as it is, is rooted in the struggles of the pioneer settlers, not only the Puritans. The need to maintain strong communities that were not riven by sexual jealousies and rivalries was paramount for survival. Communities needed to have strong leadership and individual families needed the security of a strong father. Independence from British rule only exacerbated the need for a father who represented the virtues of moral integrity and benign authority.

This deep connection between private life and public interest also reveals an underlying anxiety that pervades the American political psyche to the present day.

On a psychological level, infidelity signifies an attack on the parental couple and, consequently, on the structure of the family. When this is extended into the political arena, it represents an attack on the political leader and social structure.

Perhaps because the US was founded on the basis of a murderous rebellion against its father country, Britain, it is particularly susceptible to paranoid anxieties that its own leaders will suffer the same fate.

This is called Oedipal guilt: the guilt of the sons who want to kill the father. The fact that there have been so many assassinations and assassination attempts against the American presidency over the years seems to bear witness to this.

Ensign's confession of his sexual affair may be necessary not only to restore his own personal credibility but also to reinforce a belief in the authority and invincibility of American power, particularly at a time when the country is in a much more vulnerable position in relation to the world than perhaps it has been since the Revolution.

17 June 2009

22
Pygmalion complex of the tennis parents who can never be satisfied

This Wimbledon, there will be many parents in the audience whose sanity depends on the success of their child

"There was nothing I could ever, ever do to satisfy him, whether it's on the court, off the court." This admission came from Jelena Dokić after suffering years of abusive treatment from her father, Damir Dokić, who put her under constant pressure, criticism, and threat to become an international tennis champion.

By the age of twenty, Jelena ranked fourth in the world. Three years later, in 2006, her ranking had slipped to 621. Discouraged and brow-beaten, Jelena had stopped trying. It was only when she was able to separate from her father that she began to recover both her drive and her ranking.

Nevertheless, her father's abusive treatment of her has left its scars. Just this month, she had to withdraw from a match in Paris due to a bad back, and we are left wondering about what internal pressures may still be crippling her.

There are countless stories of pushy tennis parents and, with Wimbledon upon us, there will doubtless be more in the coming days. Damir Dokić is the most dramatic figure. He has recently been on trial in Belgrade for his threat to bomb the Australian ambassador, following Jelena's claim in an Australian magazine that he abused her as a child. Despite his protests that it was all a joke, incendiary devices and rifles were found in his home.

The Williams sisters' father, Richard Williams, is also well known for his aggressive behaviour during matches, especially aimed at his daughters' opponents. He expressed support for Jim Pierce, father of Mary, grand slam champion, who notoriously screamed at his daughter during a match, "Mary, kill the bitch!" It is perhaps no coincidence that the culprits are largely fathers—fathers who have made their child's tennis career into their own.

Most of us assume these parents are pushing their children because of unfulfilled desires and consequent frustrations of their own. While this undoubtedly plays a part in their behaviour, the story is more complex.

Some of these parents—in extreme cases—may be likened to Pygmalion. Ovid's story of Pygmalion depicts him as a sculptor who has carved a beautiful woman in ivory. Disillusioned and repelled by the sight of women prostituting themselves, Pygmalion falls in love with his perfect creation and prays to Aphrodite to bring her to life. His wish is granted, they marry, and Pygmalion's creation remains his sole possession. Although she has come to life, she is perfect partly because she is without a will and desire of her own. She is flawless and she is his.

From this myth, we can see the seeds of what in psychology is called the "Pygmalion effect", in which children perform better when their parents place high expectations on them as compared with children whose parents do not have such high expectations or have low expectations.

The parents' expectations are internalised by the child and they become a self-fulfilling prophecy. This may function in a benign way to the benefit of the child or, if the expectations are too high, it may have a destructive effect. Nothing will ever be good enough.

What is striking, for example, about Damir Dokić's abusive behaviour is that it seems to have become worse as his daughter's performance improved. Each success generates greater anxiety and the need for greater control. Not only is there more at stake, but the child's success in the mind of the parent may lessen the child's dependency. Each success brings an increased threat of independence. In Damir's case, when he lost his power over Jelena, he seems to have lost his mind.

In these extreme cases, the expectation to create perfection in the child masks a severe sense of inadequacy and failure within the parent. The often vicious attacks against the child who is not performing well enough—and against the child's opponents—are in turn an expression of sadistic rage against imperfection and failure. This rage may stem from the parent's own unconscious anger towards the parent who in turn failed them.

As the myth suggests, Pygmalion needed to create an image of a perfect woman, untarnished by failings and without her own will and her own sexuality, as an antidote to his repulsion and disillusion with women whom he associated with prostitution.

The mother who in the child's eyes has betrayed and failed him must be restored on her pedestal. But this can only happen when she is his own creation and possession. Failure in any form takes on a persecutory quality that is then lived out in the parent's need for their child to succeed.

For children like Jelena Dokić who become players in their parent's internal drama, separation from the parent becomes extremely difficult and hazardous. The child is aware at an unconscious level of the parent's mental fragility, and the need to continue to perform for the parent is inextricably linked to their need to keep the parent's mental state intact. As Jelena argues, "You can't expect a fifteen-year-old not to defend the father of your family."

Criticising her father's behaviour and failing to comply with it meant risking not only the father's sanity but the fabric of the family itself. Jelena gradually broke down in her attempts to perform for her father, and it was only when she was able to separate from him that she began to recover and he had a breakdown.

During Wimbledon fortnight, the BBC cameras will as ever pan to the parents of the young contenders. Some will appear overly eager, some just smug. However their pushiness manifests itself, when their expectations exceed what is realistic for the child, and come from their own narcissistic needs, either the child will ultimately crack or they will.

18 June 2009

23

Miscavige's reign of terror over Scientology

Brutalised staff who defected from the Church have given an insight into how its leader maintains control

"It was random and whimsical. It could be the look on your face. Or not answering a question quickly. But it always was a punishment." Mike Rinder, a Scientology spokesman for many years, described to the *St. Petersburg Times* the perverse regime of its leader, David Miscavige. Top executives from the Church have been defecting and, along with Rinder, have reported Miscavige's "gruesome" assaults and abusive behaviour towards his management team.

Miscavige adopted standard brain-washing techniques, such as sleep deprivation and intimidation, to maintain control over his executive team at their headquarters in Clearwater, Florida. Staff underwent group confessions, similar to accounts of China's Cultural Revolution, in which "bad" thoughts about Miscavige and the Church, as well as personal disclosures, including sexual fantasies, were extracted and punished. Punishments took the form of beatings and humiliation in front of the group. At times, the confessions and beatings got out of control. As one executive said: "People are wild ... I punched somebody. Everybody was punched. And screaming and yelling. It just got like, What the hell is going on here?"

The thirty or so senior Scientology staff members were permitted to leave the office only once a day for a shower. Otherwise, they remained in the office, the men slept on the floor around the conference table, women in cubicles, food was brought in, and meetings were held at arbitrary times, such as 2 a.m. or 4 a.m. Staff became physically disoriented and exhausted, barely managing to function in these conditions.

As Miscavige's reign of terror continued, it seems that his paranoia only increased and led to further attacks against staff, as well as staff attacking each other to demonstrate their loyalty to Miscavige. One member admitted attacking other staff on Miscavige's orders, explaining that it was out of a "survival instinct. If I don't attack, I'm going to be attacked." This admission is common amongst many staff and inmates alike caught within terrorist regimes, whether in the concentration camps in Germany or Cambodia, or in the prison culture or detainment camps of today.

Despite this terrifying and abusive regime and an increasing number of defections, Miscavige continues to rule over staff who either remain loyal or are so frightened that they are unable to leave. The initial attraction to a religious leader who promises narcissistic gratification to his followers—nirvana—is the seed of both the success of Miscavige's regime and its eventual downfall.

Followers are seeking the illusion of reunification with a mother—in this case personified by the Church of Scientology under the leadership of Miscavige—who makes them feel they are the centre of her world and who will eradicate the frustrations and failings in life.

This very powerful and seductive illusion offers a magical solution to life's obstacles and limitations in return for complete loyalty and abnegation of having a mind and personality of one's own. It is the regressive world of the mother where there is no separation between baby and mother. It is the antithesis of the world of the father and the real leader who depends on the resources and minds of his followers to help the group to grow and to develop, to overcome and work through problems rather than to magically deny them.

Most groups that function well are not based on an illusory ideal. When the real leader goes astray, there are other options to ensure the group's survival. Other leaders may step in or other managers will take over to enable the group to continue to function. The basic structure of the group remains relatively intact so that it does not fall apart in these situations and the followers remain protected to a considerable degree.

In a group based on illusion, there is no independent structure. The leader is the structure, and this is often why so many cult groups end up destroying themselves. The psychological pressure on the leader to maintain his omnipotent position is enormous, and the more this fails, as it inevitably does in the face of reality, the more the leader is backed into a corner. Rule by tyranny ultimately leads to group suicide. This was tragically demonstrated by the Jonestown mass suicide, to name but one example.

The executive staff who defected from Miscavige's regime have had the courage to give up the illusion offered by Miscavige and to acknowledge its perversity as well as their own collusion in it. For those who remain, the thought of defection—and the admission that they were deluded—may simply be too painful.

26 June 2009

24

Narcissistic obsessions killed the Man in the Mirror

Whether or not drugs were involved, it was Michael Jackson's obsession with his appearance that ultimately killed him

Surrounded by his entourage of "enablers" in his hospital bed in the UCLA Medical Centre, Michael Jackson died last Friday with his music playing and "bouncing off the walls". Jackson was to the end a performer, transfixed with seeing himself and hearing himself, with being seen and being heard, searching for the public limelight and for the reassurance of being loved by all.

One nine-year-old boy, in tears when he heard of Jackson's death, explained that he was crying because no one stopped Michael Jackson from continuing to have plastic surgery and this is what killed him. In some important respect, this is true.

Although it is alleged that Jackson died of his addiction to Demerol and the cocktail of painkillers he took regularly, his obsession with his image drove him to extremes of medical intervention. If anyone had tried to stop Jackson from further plastic surgery or another round of prescriptions for pain-relievers, they had clearly failed to be heard.

Like Narcissus looking longingly into the pool at his reflection, Jackson could only see his own image in the eyes of others. The reflected image, however, can never reach out and make the viewer feel wanted, it can never have a life of its own, it can never give the love of another.

According to Ovid's story of Narcissus, the river god Cephisus seduced the nymph Leirope, who gave birth to the beautiful Narcissus. Concerned about his future, Leirope was told by the prophet Teiresias that he would come to no harm as long as he did not know himself.

By the age of sixteen, Narcissus arrogantly spurns the advances of numerous suitors, including the nymph Echo who cannot address him directly but can only repeat what he says. Pining for his love, Echo is heartbroken and wastes away until only her voice remains.

Aware of her suffering, the god Nemesis condemns Narcissus to a similar fate of unrequited love. Coming upon a pool of water, the thirsty Narcissus drinks, falls in love with his reflection, and, unable to bear the pain of not being responded to, kills himself.

Tragically, Jackson's life imitated myth. His striving to obtain love from the reflected pool of an anonymous audience was doomed to fail. Just as there was no real person who could reflect reality back to Narcissus and rescue him from his unrequited love, there was no concerned father who could provide a mirror for Jackson's self-destructive behaviour and stop him from killing himself.

Unlike Narcissus, who never knew his father, Jackson's father Joe, a failed rhythm 'n' blues singer, was very much in evidence. Jackson's mother, who suffered from polio-related disabilities throughout her life, was also musical. However, it was Joe who was determined—out of his own narcissistic failure—to transform their five boys into star performers, and Michael, the youngest and most talented, stole the show from the age of six.

Like many parents of star performers, Joe Jackson brutalised his children by imposing exhausting work schedules and sadistically bullying them into perfecting their musical routines. Michael

Jackson admitted to Oprah Winfrey that he would sometimes feel sick from fear at the sight of his father.

What seems to have been especially traumatic to Jackson as a child was his father's nickname for him: "Big Nose". He subsequently had so many nose jobs that after a point, his surgeons dared not risk another one and began to fake them, persuading Jackson that they had done further surgery when they had not.

For Jackson, the persistent pressure to perform at the top of his ability, and to perfect his image to conform to some idealised icon he had in his mind, were powerful indicators of his desperate longing to be loved by a father who had made him feel he could never get it right.

Michael Jackson's face changed from being that of a black African-American boy to looking like a Hollywood female starlet, with a markedly slim nose, white skin, and a dimple on his chin. Some photographs make Jackson look remarkably similar to such female stars as Elizabeth Taylor and Liza Minelli, both of whom he was close to and admired.

There was an uncanny sense that Jackson was trying to slip into the body of a woman. It has also been rumoured that Jackson was on hormone treatment to preserve his high falsetto voice. His increasingly feminine appearance suggests that he may have felt, at least at an unconscious level, that he could only have really been loved by his father if he had been a girl.

At a deeper level, Jackson may also have come close to resembling a woman as a way of trying to be inside his mother's body—a mother who had not perhaps been able to make him feel she was able to keep him inside her mind.

Jackson's attempts to transform his physical appearance were also bound up with his terror of ageing. While Jackson took other extreme measures not to age, such as sleeping in an oxygen tent, his emotional development seems to have remained fixed at the point of his sudden stardom.

Walter Yetnikoff, head of CBS Records, who bought the Jackson Five from Motown, recalled: "He had no social skills. Sometimes I felt that he was still six." Although Jackson was not sixteen, like Narcissus, he encountered his nemesis when he was discovered by an adoring public.

Perhaps the saddest and most telling relationship Jackson managed to have in the course of his life was with his pet chimpanzee, Bubbles, whom he adopted in 1986 and treated much as a baby or a baby extension of himself.

The well-known pioneer of French psychoanalysis Jacques Lacan once referred to his dog, Justine, as the only one who never took him for another. By this, he meant that his dog did not expect him to be anything other than what he was, and was therefore the only one who made him feel truly loved.

We can imagine that Bubbles, like Justine, may have been the only one for whom Jackson did not feel he had to wear a mask or perform in order to be loved. Humans, in his experience, loved him for the star they wanted him to be, and his desire to fulfil this role played a major part in his premature death at the age of fifty.

Jackson's incessant quest to transform himself into a public idol in order to find the love that he was yearning for may yet ultimately—and ironically—succeed.

The German doctor Gunther von Hagens was said to have been in talks with Jackson months before his death to preserve his body as a "plastinated" mummy, to be placed next to his beloved Bubbles, who was plastinated a number of years ago, to live on forever together.

29 June 2009

25

Antichrist director Lars von Trier plays god to create a new morality

The controversial film can be read as episodes based on von Trier's fantasies stemming from his early relationships with his own parents

"I don't have a choice … It's the hand of God, I'm afraid. And I am the best film director in the world. I'm not sure God is the best god in the world." This was Lars von Trier's answer when asked to justify his latest controversial, sexually explicit, and violent film, *Antichrist*, on release from today.

Von Trier has no inhibition about announcing he is the best film director in the world—something that might suggest a touch of the omnipotent antichrist who in the next breath compares himself to God and questions God's ability to do his job. And yet, this is precisely what von Trier's film is about, leaving us ultimately in an upside-down world ruled by Rational Thought and destructiveness.

The plot of *Antichrist* is simple enough. We enter the bathroom of an apartment where we see, graphically portrayed, a young couple making love, their passion reflected in the chaotic spin of the washing machine behind them. In a child's bedroom, a window blows open and heavy snowflakes begin to float through the air. The couple's toddler son wakes up, is enchanted by the snow, gets out of bed, opens the baby gate separating him from his parents, and spies them making love. He turns to the camera smiling, like a small god.

The toddler retraces his steps to the open window of his bedroom where he shows his teddy the snowflakes, climbs onto the ledge, and he and his teddy leap out the window to their death on the pavement below. The toddler's expression as he falls is striking and gives the impression that he is having a fantasy of flying or being one of the snowdrops—he appears ecstatic and calm as he descends in slow motion.

The rest of the film is the story of the mother's (Charlotte Gainsbourg) inconsolable guilt and grief, and her psychologist husband's (Willem Dafoe) attempts to heal her by means of "exposure" therapy in which he encourages her to confront her fears in order to discover that they do not exist in reality.

As the husband's need to control his wife's emotions becomes evident, so does her passive hatred of him. He takes her back to Eden, the cottage in the forest where she had spent time alone with her son and seems to represent the place in which she first becomes aware of her own unhappiness. "She", as the wife/mother is called, is compliant, and masochistically accepts her husband's control.

The hatred between them emerges as they enter into an increasingly sadistic struggle in which sex and violence are used as palliatives to grief. "She" finally breaks and savagely attacks her husband's genitals and then, when "He" is unconscious, crucifies him by pinning a drill through his leg. "He" becomes the Antichrist. "She" then cuts off her clitoris in an act of self-castration that highlights her emotional castration. In the end, "She" is strangled by her husband in a scene that evokes the violence of their love-making.

Von Trier wrote the script for *Antichrist* in the midst of a crippling depression for which he was receiving cognitive therapy.

He confesses he felt "no pleasure in doing this film" and ventures no ideas as to what the film signifies. However, there is a powerful sense in the film that von Trier is working out some inner drama that gives the film its haunting, dream-like quality.

Von Trier's picture of his childhood is bleak and lonely. His parents were civil servants who rebelled against authority and rules. They were committed to communism, atheism, and nudism. They also did not believe in telling their son what to do as a child, when to go to bed, etc., and it seems he was left to his own devices much of the time.

"I could do more or less what I wanted", he says. The effect of this was to leave von Trier anxious and frightened of the world around him, a world of chaos in which he had to stave off disaster by obsessionally controlling his objects. His role as film director has enabled von Trier to maintain some illusion of being able to control the objects and people in his world. He can be God on the film-set world of his creation.

Von Trier does not seem to have recovered fully from his breakdown following his mother's death in 1995. On her death-bed, his mother disclosed the fact that the father he had grown up with until his death, when von Trier was eighteen, was not his real father, and that she had chosen instead a Roman Catholic composer to be his biological father in the hope that her son would inherit his artistic genes.

Von Trier converted to Catholicism, explaining that it was partly "to piss off a few of my countrymen (mostly protestant)". He suffered a further blow when his biological father refused to see him, stipulating that "we can talk through my lawyer".

The deception about his origins and the confusion of growing up in a world in which authority was suspect and to be shunned come through as strong themes in *Antichrist*. The mother is aware that her toddler son has been waking in the night recently and can open the baby gate, yet she never mentions this to her husband, nor does she take precautions to secure the baby gate.

The toddler is left free to roam and when he discovers his parents making love, he smiles triumphantly in his new-found power over them. His leap to his death, and the subsequent trials and sufferings of his parents, follow on from this scene.

The entire film can be read as episodes from von Trier's fantasies stemming from his early relationships. Excluded from mother by father, the little boy kills himself in order to punish his mother for her infidelity.

In this way, he can live on in her mind forever, he can forever come between the couple, and he can also have mother to himself in death.

While von Trier has been accused repeatedly of being a misogynist, the prevailing sense in *Antichrist* is his emotional identification and empathy with the mother along with the desire to possess and control her, as played out by the father.

It is the father, the wooden psychologist whom the mother accuses of being arrogant and believing he is better than the doctors treating her, who is depicted as unable to feel and who is reviled. The father has been a distant husband and a distant father, who is terrified of emotions. He eschews psychic reality in favour of rational thought, and this is where the film becomes more than simply a biographical narrative or a story of Oedipal revenge.

Von Trier has created a modern-day morality play, situated in the Garden of Eden (the place where the troubles begin). What unfolds is a lethal fight between Rational Thinking, as represented by the husband, and Nature, as represented by the wife.

The therapist husband consistently denies his wife's psychic reality, her fantasies and feelings, and insists that only what is concrete is real. He asserts, "Good and evil have nothing to do with therapy". To which his wife sardonically replies, "Freud is dead".

Rational Thinking attacks Nature because it cannot be controlled, like the unconscious.

"She" aligns herself with Nature. "She" explains that because women cannot control their bodies, they are subject to Nature. When "She" makes this clear to her husband, he replies by stating that he wants to hurt her, Nature, as much as he can. "She" says, "By frightening me", and "He" corrects her and says, "By killing you".

"He" cannot bear to be out of control. What is of paramount importance is that the world is ordered, and this negates any need to differentiate between good and evil. While good and evil do not exist for the psychotherapist husband, they are clearly manifest within his wife, who struggles with a growing awareness of her own destructiveness and guilt.

In the end, it is precisely this conflict that is killed by Rational Thinking. The final scene depicts the husband, leaving Eden, hobbling on a crutch through a desiccated landscape where Nature has been destroyed. It is the final triumph of Rationality, the Antichrist, and the hills are suddenly swarming with pilgrims advancing towards their new God.

Von Trier's struggle to control the feelings and impulses of his own inner world are undoubtedly played out through the device of the morality play. But the final message is a bleak warning of the dangers of trying to control Nature and unconscious processes.

In its horror, the film conveys a deep sense of morality and, as its maker, von Trier is less of an Antichrist than he is a Trickster— a god who disturbs the order of things, who challenges the boundaries and crosses borders in order to create an awareness of a different reality.

24 July 2009

26

Madness of wanting to be normal: Nancy Garrido's make-believe family

Wife of sex offender Phillip Garrido had powerful capacity for denial

In his first ninety-minute interview with Nancy Garrido, the wife of Phillip Garrido, her lawyer Gilbert Maines reported: "She has said to me she misses the girls, that she loves them and her feeling was they had become a family. They acted like a family. It seems strange given the circumstances but that's it. She's distraught, frightened, and appeared to be a little lost."

The "circumstances" Maines refers to are the discovery last week that Phillip and Nancy Garrido had abducted eleven-year-old Jaycee Lee Dugard in South Lake Tahoe in 1991, and held her captive in ramshackle tents and sheds at the bottom of their Californian garden.

The "family" consists of Jaycee Lee Dugard's two daughters, fifteen-year-old Starlet and eleven-year-old Angel, fathered by Phillip Garrido and raised as if they were Nancy's children and Jaycee Lee Dugard was their older sister.

The dispute now is whether Nancy was a victim of what Maines describes as her husband's "suppressive control" or whether she was a willing accomplice. Whatever the ultimate verdict, Nancy is named in the twenty-nine felony charges, including forcible rape, that have been made against her husband and herself.

Neighbours describe Nancy as very quiet, depressed, and anxious-looking, and in the shadow of her husband, deferring to him when asked any questions. Phillip Garrido's brother described Nancy as a "robot" who was "under his [brother's] spell" and would do "anything he asked".

There seems to be no doubt that Nancy's compliance towards her husband was extreme. There is also a striking resemblance between Nancy's "robotic" mindlessness and the mindlessness presented by the two daughters, who had never gone to school, never seen a doctor, and were rarely seen outside their sound-proofed tent.

This mindlessness was maintained within the restricted family environment that allowed only minimal contact with the outside world. Typical to children who have grown up being abused, this was their only experience of being in a family and being cared for, and, as such, perceived as "normal".

On the other hand, Jaycee Lee Dugard had not grown up in this kind of environment and was forced to assimilate the madness of her new environment in order to survive both physically and mentally. While Jaycee Lee Dugard was "brainwashed", as a new member of a tyrannical and perverse regime, her daughters, and possibly Nancy, had never known anything different.

Nancy is thought to have been actively involved in Jaycee's abduction and subsequent incarceration. She is suspected of being in the car and physically kidnapping Dugard while her husband was driving. She witnessed her husband's sexual abuse of Dugard, and she assisted in the birth of Dugard's two daughters. Her defence will undoubtedly argue that she was a "victim" of her husband's tyranny.

The prosecution, however, is expected to argue that Nancy's actions were complicit and not a result of her victimisation. They are expected to focus on a period in 1993 when Phillip Garrido was locked up in federal custody for an unspecified parole violation for thirty-eight days. This was a time, it could be argued, when Nancy could have freed Dugard, but instead she continued to keep her captive.

Although the defence might argue in turn that Nancy was too terrified of the consequences of freeing Dugard, it is nevertheless conceivable that this option may never have occurred to her because of her own need to keep up appearances of having a "normal" family.

We know very little about Nancy Garrido's childhood and family background. We do know that it was during a visit to her uncle, who was an inmate at Levenworth prison in Kansas, that she met another inmate, Phillip Garrido. She must have known that Phillip was near to being released early from serving the fifty-year prison sentence he had been issued for the rape and abduction of a twenty-five-year-old casino waitress in Reno, Nevada, in 1977.

Nancy and Phillip married in 1988, when he was still behind bars. While Phillip may have used his marriage as leverage with the prison authorities to demonstrate his rehabilitation, it is also possible that both Phillip and Nancy shared a fantasy of establishing what appeared to be a normal life and family, having most likely come from extremely dysfunctional families themselves.

The fact that Nancy chose to marry a man with this kind of criminal record indicates that she had a powerful capacity for denial long before any of the events that followed. It also suggests that she was masochistically attracted to a man who would abuse her and enlist her as an accomplice in abusing others.

Joining forces with the abuser is often, perversely, a way of feeling loved and special. The couple can form a world of their own above and beyond the limits of reality, so they don't have to be aware of their own inadequacies and their own deprivation.

It is not clear why Nancy and Phillip never had their own children, as Nancy was thirty-three when they married. Either she was unable to conceive or there was some psychological prohibition that prevented them from having children. Whatever it was, the abduction of Dugard and the two daughters that were later conceived by her produced a ready-made family for the Garridos: a family that in certain respects enabled them to appear, at least in their minds, like everyone else.

People who have suffered extreme abuse will often go to extreme lengths to create a life that on the surface appears to be normal in an attempt to hide the shame, the hatred, and the terror of their past from others and from themselves. However, the tragedy is that underneath this surface, the abuse is re-enacted with the next generation.

Nancy's lawyer described her as "a little lost" and as a boat "without a rudder". Like her husband, she is now under suicide watch pending trial. The make-believe family Nancy and Phillip had constructed has now unravelled perilously, exposing the stark reality of the madness that has destroyed their lives.

4 September 2009

27

What Hitler and Aids have in common

The shocking German ad that uses Hitler as a metaphor for Aids is a stroke of genius

Warning: Video contains graphic sexual images. A couple, in the throes of passion, rip each other's clothes off, and with unbridled lust, they plunge into bed together. We have not seen the man's face and, suddenly, as he climaxes, he lifts his face to the camera and it is *Adolf Hitler, grinning with triumph*. This is the video just released in Germany, created for an Aids-awareness organisation by the Hamburg advertising agency Das Committee.

Aids organisations across Europe are up in arms, criticising the campaign on the grounds that it can only further stigmatise Aids sufferers. But giving Aids the face of Hitler is not just a shock tactic, it is a brilliant metaphor for the silent, creeping spread of a disease that is destroying whole populations in Africa and Asia and mortally infecting huge numbers of men and women in Europe and the US. It is a modern-day plague, but a plague that we have the knowledge and means to control. It is therefore even more curious that it is spreading and not contracting.

When Hitler rose to power, he personified an omnipotent ideal who had ultimate authority and promised his followers, like other tyrants, a paradisiacal return to a pure state in which there would be no strife, no deprivation, and racial supremacy that ensured no enemies. The state would, seemingly, take care of all its members as a perfect mother would take care of her children. This ideal, cloaked in the guise of purity and love, gave rise to the mass exterminations of those who were "other" and a threat to the ideology.

There is a striking similarity in the mentality that lies behind much of the spread of Aids now. At its most extreme, French radio reported a recent phenomenon of sex parties in which healthy people come together with Aids carriers for sex. No one knows who is infected and who is not, so the excitement is in the game of Russian roulette. The person who takes part in unprotected sex knows he or she is taking a risk and defies the odds. It is a mentality that transcends the need for protection, that defies death while courting it, and that expresses contempt for vulnerability and weakness.

The sexual intercourse that may be mistaken for love is in fact imbued with a disregard and hatred of the "other" and oneself. If some of the sexual partners are caught in the crossfire of unprotected sex, they become martyrs to the cause at least at an unconscious level. They have sacrificed their life in the service of an omnipotent god who will honour their fight against weakness in death.

Followers of a tyrannical regime are required to subjugate their will to their leader in order to safeguard the total power of the regime. The regime promises a return to the perfect world of infancy, being at one with the world—at the cost of the individual. Ultimately, it is a death wish that negates the frustrations and pain of reality, much like a moth attracted to a flame.

The appeal of having unprotected sex is the excitement of killing consciousness and embracing omnipotence. Hitler also offered this appeal, ultimately leading his country into a dance with death.

11 September 2009

28

Why the world is scared of hermaphrodites

Ambiguous gender identity in another can trigger anxieties about our own unconscious homosexual fantasies

"I see it all as a joke, it doesn't upset me. God made me the way I am and I accept myself." This was Caster Semenya's response to accusations made following her exceptional victory in the women's 800-metre final at the recent world athletics championships that she is a man, not a woman.

However, Semenya made this statement when she was convinced she was a woman. Now it seems the facts are not so clear, and leaked medical tests, conducted under the aegis of the International Association of Athletics Federations, indicate that the eighteen-year-old South African winner has both male and female sexual characteristics. The "joke" has turned nasty. Semenya has been transformed from star to monster in the eyes of the world—seen, mistakenly, as neither man nor woman but as hermaphrodite.

The controversy within the professional world of competitive sports centres on the crucial division between men's and women's sports—an historical distinction intended to recognise differences in physical strength and capabilities between the sexes. So far, so good, but what happens when these differences are not so clear-cut?

113

The sports world is a microcosm of the world at large—the confusion and fiery passions surrounding gender ambiguity touch a raw nerve that reverberates within each of our psyches and throughout our society.

When the distinction is clear between who is a man and who is a woman, we know how to relate to each other. When this distinction is blurred or eroded, we become anxious and disorientated.

A "true" hermaphrodite, that is, an organism born with a complete set of male and female sexual organs, exists only among other species such as the earthworm. The gender of humans is determined by the development of the gonads within the embryo. Because we are born with one set of gonads, this means that despite abnormalities in development, our sexual characteristics are either male or female. In normal female development, the gonads will become ovaries, the female genitalia will enlarge, and the male genitalia will recede. The opposite occurs in the case of male development. To describe a person as a "true" hermaphrodite is therefore a misnomer. The correct term is either a "pseudo-hermaphrodite" or, in its politicised form, an "intersex".

In instances of sexual ambiguity, gender is ultimately determined by the internal characteristics of the gonads. A male hermaphrodite is identified by the presence of internal testes, and a female hermaphrodite has internal ovaries, regardless of external genitalia. Every so-called hermaphrodite has a gender, although someone's appearance may belie it. What is intolerable in our minds is sexual ambiguity.

Despite the reality that there is no such thing as a "hermaphrodite" among humans, the possibility of embodying both sexes is a powerful fantasy. The image of the hermaphrodite that is prevalent in so many religions symbolises spiritual unity between opposites and completeness or inner harmony.

On a more primitive level, the hermaphrodite fascinates us because it transcends sexual difference and holds out the illusion of being able to experience what it is like to be the opposite sex—one of the greatest mysteries of our lives.

While the symbol of the hermaphrodite is fascinating because it breaks the boundaries of nature, its reality is horrifying for the same reasons. Gender identity provides us with the most basic guide as to how we relate to others, while it also affects the way in which we experience ourselves and our own gender identity.

When gender identity is ambiguous in someone else, it challenges our conceptions of who we are. It can also trigger anxieties about our own unconscious homosexual fantasies. The hermaphrodite exists outside our gender assumptions and expectations, and this is what is so very disturbing.

Our core identity is based on gender. The first question asked about a newborn baby is its sex. When this is in doubt or equivocal, it is like losing one's internal compass or seeing an indeterminate being in the mirror.

The hermaphrodite confronts us with the fact that our gender is inextricably tied up with our feelings of potency—whether we call ourselves men or women. It makes us fearful of losing our potency and sense of self and of being taken over by what may feel like an alien other within us. Being without gender has the makings of madness.

This is very different from the homosexual, transvestite, or transsexual who normally has a clear sense of his gender identity even when it may not correspond to what he looks like.

According to the leaked reports, Semenya's test results indicate that she has internal testes and this means, strictly speaking, "she" qualifies as a "he". Not only is she being hounded off the running track by her opponents, but she is being told that she is not the young woman she thought she was.

It is hardly surprising that she has gone into hiding and is being given counselling for trauma. The discovery that her gender is by no means clear places Semenya in a transitional role, no longer able to claim she is a woman and yet unable to be a man. She has to make sense of the incongruity that she is now faced with between her body, now classified as male, and her mental experience of being a woman.

While her supporters, including the American gold medallist Carl Lewis, are decrying how unprotected Semenya has been, her strength will undoubtedly lie in her experience of how she was loved as an infant and in how secure her mother felt as a woman.

If she is in fact able to accept herself as she says, she will be able to weather this ordeal and be a champion in a larger arena. She has certainly made us all aware that the assignment of gender identity is something that is conferred and constructed—it is not simply a biological given.

17 September 2009

29

The fear behind Japan's flourishing rent-a-friend business

More and more Japanese are employing fake friends and bosses in order to save face

"In three and a half years, I've never once been caught out", says Ryuichi Ichinokawa, founder of Tokyo-based Office Agents, one of the "rent-a-friend" businesses currently flourishing in Japan.

Ichinokawa makes sure his "agents"—available for hire as "friends", "work colleagues", and even "relatives"—know the answers to every possible question in advance. A slip could ruin the reputation of his client and his business.

Business is booming. After four years, Ichinokawa now employs thirty agents and charges £150 for wedding appearances, or more if the agent is asked to speak or sing karaoke. The economic recession has increased demand as requests come in for agents to act as "bosses" or "work colleagues" to cover up for the fact that the client has, in fact, lost his or her job.

In short, the need to save face in public is a growing concern amongst the Japanese. The roles agents are asked to play range from being best man at a wedding, to being a child's "uncle" at a sports event, to being a parent attending a match-making party. They might be asked to be a husband at a social gathering, or even a rival suitor. What each situation has in common is that the client wants the agent to fill in the gap in his or her life—a gap they feel unable to broach publicly.

Behind the example of the "uncle" watching his nephew's sports event is the fact that the child's mother is a divorcee, the father is absent, and the son is being bullied at school by his peers. It is clear that the divorcee is attempting to fill in the gap of her missing husband and her son's missing father in the hope, apart from anything else, that this will solve the problem of her son being bullied.

The "uncle" is also a stand-in father and, at least in the mother's mind, will quite literally represent the protective authority figure that is missing in their lives.

Another situation described by Ichinokawa is acting to rescue love affairs that are failing. A woman client employs an agent to act as a potential rival in order to re-kindle her lover's interest. When she is in public with her inattentive boyfriend, the agent is programmed to "accidentally" turn up, show that they've met before and express overt interest in her. Here, the agent is asked to collude with the woman in trying to cover up the fact that her boyfriend has lost interest in her, if he was ever interested in the first place.

Whatever role the agent is asked to play points to an underlying emotional gap in the client that is too painful to know about— much less risk exposing. Hiring a "boss" might be the most obvious attempt at saving face, but there are invariably deeper emotional gaps that agents are being asked to fill.

In a culture that prides itself on the importance of form and structure, on putting on a good public appearance—it is perhaps especially shameful when the facts of one's life don't correspond to how they are supposed to be. For many people, these discrepancies convey a terrible sense of failure and inadequacy. Having to hire friends and relatives only highlights the isolation of Ichinokawa's clients and how much intimacy is lacking in their lives.

Japan is a culture known during the Second World War for its kamikaze pilots, but which now has an extreme fear of vulnerability and defeat.

It is ironic that Ichinokawa originally wanted to train as a counsellor. Instead of training, he set up his agency and now claims that what he is providing is a kind of counselling.

However, in helping clients cover up their problems, the agents seem to be acting more in the role of social prostitutes, giving short-term relief that must be kept secret at all costs. Creating the façade of a life without problems is immensely seductive, but it is the client who is fooled in the end.

25 September 2009

30

What were Geimer and Shields' mothers thinking?

**Samantha Geimer and Brooke Shields satisfied
their mothers' fantasies of seducing father and
getting rid of mother**

"So I fucked a chick? So what?" This was Roman Polanski's
response to Thomas Kiernan, author of *The Roman Polanski Story*,
when questioned about his rape of Samantha Geimer in 1977.
According to Kiernan, Polanski was notorious for his sexual interest in "*very* young girls"—making a public display of his spell over
them.

While this is something that Samantha Geimer's aspiring
mother may not have been aware of—unlikely as that may seem—
she was the one who introduced Samantha, at the age of thirteen,
to Polanski in order to further her daughter's modelling career.
Polanski had been asked to guest edit an edition of French *Vogue*
and wanted to feature Geimer. The bait was set.

Polanski wasted no time. During Geimer's first photoshoot—
at *her* home—he asked her to remove her clothes as he photographed her. Only two weeks later, Geimer's mother allowed her to
be taken to a private photoshoot with Polanski. Although Polanski
had promised to bring one of Geimer's friends along as a chaperone, he failed to do so. Geimer went alone with Polanski. After
several glasses of champagne, Polanski suggested that Geimer
once again remove her clothes so he could photograph her in the

bath. When Geimer resisted his sexual approaches, he gave her a sedative and raped her while she was unconscious.

Where was Geimer's mother throughout this time? It is strange that she was not present at the first photoshoot, that she allowed a second photoshoot to take place without her being there, and, seemingly, did not check to see that her daughter was in fact accompanied by a chaperone. Geimer's mother's failure to take protective measures towards her daughter suggests more than turning a blind eye; it suggests her complicity—even if it was unconscious. All of this in the guise of helping her daughter's career?

Geimer later sued Polanski, winning an undisclosed settlement, and now wants the case to be put to rest. She pleads, "Every time this case is brought to the attention of the court, great focus is made of me, my family, my mother, and others. That attention is not pleasant to experience and is not worth maintaining over some irrelevant legal nicety, the continuation of the case."

It is understandable that Geimer, now forty-five and a mother of three, does not want to relive her trauma in the courts. It must be difficult for her to avoid questioning her mother's role in what happened and to what extent her mother might have been to blame for her being sexually abused.

While Hollywood is divided as to whether or not Polanski should be brought back to trial, in London, the Tate Modern, following police orders, has had to withdraw a *provocative photograph of Brooke Shields* from its new show, *Pop Life*.

The photograph, by the American artist Richard Prince, is of another photograph, taken by a commercial photographer, Gary Gross, in 1975. The Prince photograph, ironically titled "Spiritual America", shows Brooke Shields, aged ten, standing naked in a bath, her face heavily made up and her torso gleamingly oiled. Children's campaigners fear that the photograph is a magnet for paedophiles. Of even greater concern is the fact that Shields, at the age of ten, could not have given informed consent.

Shields's mother, like Geimer's, played an important part behind the scenes of the original photograph. She commissioned Gross to take it, intent on making her daughter into a film star. She then signed away the rights to the negatives and the photograph later featured in a Playboy Press publication.

In this case, Shields's mother, Teri, could not argue that she had no idea what was going on—she had set it up. And she did not stop there. The following year, when Brooke was still eleven, she began filming *Pretty Baby*, Louis Malle's movie about a child prostitute.

By 1980, aged fifteen, she was in *The Blue Lagoon*, controversial for its many nude scenes, and appearing in *advertisements across America selling Calvin Klein jeans*, with the provocative line: "You wanna know what comes between me and my Calvins? Nothing." Throughout this period, Teri Shields continued to be the driving force behind her daughter's rising stardom.

Both mothers were driven to turn their daughters into stars at any cost. Financial motivation seemed to be secondary to narcissistic gain. Both mothers encouraged their daughters to be depicted as nymphettes who could seduce men with their pubescent or prepubescent sexuality.

Both daughters played out parts in their mothers' fantasies that may well have fitted in with their own fantasies. There was also the perverse excitement of being put into the hands of an abusive father figure.

As Lolitas, the daughters could vicariously satisfy their mothers' fantasies of seducing father and getting rid of mother. At the same time, the daughters could also enact their own fantasy of seducing father—with mother's permission.

What is evident in both scenarios is that the need for a protective mother is denied. The role played by the mother is virtually an empty one. There is no mindful mother present. In reality, both mothers did fail to think about their daughters' needs, suggesting in turn that they too had been failed by their mothers.

Richard Prince commented that the image of Brooke Shields in "Spiritual America" represented an "abstract entity". This is a haunting description of what both daughters became for their mothers and, indeed, what their mothers also became—abstract entities, seemingly without human feeling and thought.

2 October 2009

31

Women paedophiles come out of hiding

We should not be surprised that women are sex abusers too

"I would plead to her, tell those parents, all those parents who want to know." This is Vanessa George's husband Andrew begging his wife to name the children she has admitted to sexually abusing while she was employed as a nursery-school worker in Plymouth.

Vanessa George, along with Angela Allen from Nottingham and Colin Blanchard from Rochdale, pleaded guilty in court last week to sexually abusing young children.

Aged thirty-nine, and with two daughters of her own, she had worked at Little Ted's nursery school for nearly a decade. She was well liked by the mothers, who described her as "a big bubbly woman … friendly, lovely, absolutely lovely. The kids love her." Some regarded her as a "second mother".

Today, those same parents refer to her as a "monster"; the sight of her makes them feel sick—after George's sexual activities came to light by chance when a colleague of Colin Blanchard's came across disturbing images of young children on Blanchard's computer and reported him to the police.

The trail led to Vanessa George and Angela Allen who had met on Facebook and for two years had been exchanging sexual images of children, including photographs George had taken.

Their internet sexual activities and excitement grew to the point where they began to suggest the possibility of abducting young children for sexual purposes.

George was charged with assault on a girl aged around one, "touching" another infant girl, a serious assault on an infant boy, and a further serious sexual assault on an infant girl. In addition, she was charged with the possession and distribution of indecent images of children.

What is so shocking and disturbing about the case is the fact that a woman who was entrusted with the care of small children could do such a thing.

Paedophiles are most commonly thought of as being men, but as more and more cases like George and Allen come to light, women are entering the statistics as recognised paedophiles. The Lucy Faithfull Foundation (LFF), a British child protection charity that deals with female sex offenders, estimates that as many as twenty per cent of Britain's 320,000 suspected paedophiles are women.

Women suspected of committing sexual offences have traditionally been treated differently by the criminal justice system, often being referred on to social services or welfare agencies for treatment. While male paedophiles tend to be viewed as predators, female paedophiles have in the past been regarded as mentally ill. When cases involving women offenders do go to court, they are often referred to family court for trial and are not reported because of confidentiality restrictions.

What has also led us to assume that women abusers are a rarity is that there is less reporting of sexual abuse by women. In their role as caregivers, women, like George, are the least suspected and the most hidden. Sexual abuses occur most typically against their own children, relatives, or with other children in their care. Many of the children are too young to be able to know what is being done to them, much less to complain about it. Older children may feel too guilty, ashamed, or, in the case of boys, emasculated to report it.

There is a striking similarity here with findings relating to incest between mothers and their sons. Research suggests that the incidence of mother–son incest is far greater than we might imagine it to be. Again, there are various reasons why it is not discovered: if the mother is a single parent, it is less likely to be spotted by a fellow adult. Then there is the nature of the behaviour—say, bathing an eleven-year-old child: this would be considered abusive if carried out by a father, but merely eccentric or abnormal if done by a mother. And whatever the precise nature of the abuse, if it started at an early age, it is likely to be regarded as "normal" by the child. In the case of abused teenagers, the incest becomes apparent when the girl becomes pregnant. With a boy, there is no such giveaway sign.

The myth that women are not involved in child sexual abuse is being challenged with the explosion of internet child pornography and the high number of women users involved.

Given that girls are just as likely, if not more likely, as boys to be abused by parents physically, sexually, or emotionally, it is not surprising that as adults they may be vulnerable to repeating this abuse. Those who treat child sex abusers claim that "women are capable of terrible crimes against children, just as bad as men".

In the case of Vanessa George, we know that she had been increasingly estranged from her husband, whom she married in 1993, and was looking for excitement. Her husband claims he knew nothing of her sexual activities and is now divorcing her.

George[1]'s mother died when she was thirty-seven, of breast cancer, leaving George, at the age of fifteen, "devastated". Her tie to her mother was so strong that she became involved in paranormal groups and regularly attended seances to try to make contact.

Vanessa George's need for more and more excitement suggests that the paedophile activities had become her way of holding herself together mentally, as an unconscious escape from what may have been her own abuse as a child at the hands of her own mother.

Patterns of abuse are repeated in precise ways, and George is likely to have experienced some form of eroticised contact with her mother when she was very young. The abuse is perceived by the child as love, not as something hateful. This is why so many paedophiles believe they are doing nothing wrong with a child.

For George, her sexual contact with young children may have been not only her way of loving them but of tying them to her emotionally, so that they would be in her thrall through their own fear and excitement. George was like a "second mother"—but a mother who could not differentiate love from hate. It is likely that she needed to blur the distinction so that she would not have to face the horror of what had happened to her and how to live with that.

Her need to keep in contact with her dead mother is perhaps a sign of her desperation to keep alive the illusion of a loving mother within herself.

5 October 2009

32

The new trend in beards raises awkward questions

Women don't like beards, so who are men growing them for—and why?

Facial hair is "in" for men. Designer stubble has grown into the designer beard. The list of men in the limelight who now have full beards has skyrocketed. Top of the list are David Beckham, Brad Pitt, Sting, Johnny Depp, and Michael Sheen.

One explanation for the trend is that it is a good way of hiding from the paparazzi. Big bushy beards are best for this purpose, but also signify "I don't work in an office" along with a back-to-nature look that appeals to the environmentalists. Whatever it is that motivates men to grow their own, the trend does raise questions about what is happening to men in our culture, and why this sudden assertion of masculinity?

It seems no coincidence that beards are on the rise at a time when the West is struggling with a world recession and the position of powerful men is under threat. It is arguably much tougher these days to be an alpha male, and what better way to stand out than with a beard? After all, the beard is a man's follicular armour and provides a visual display of physical strength and stature.

It is also a common way for men to hide their vulnerability. Men will often grow beards when they have suffered a bereavement, a trauma such as divorce or job loss, or an injury. Young men tend to grow beards in order to look older and to give them gravitas.

There is also an increasing awareness in the West of powerful women in all spheres of life. There is not only the alpha female who is fast becoming a rival to the alpha male, especially in business, politics, and the arts, but there is the new image of the "cougar", the female equivalent of the playboy, to contend with. The tables have turned, and the cougar preys on the "pretty boys" who become her "arm candy". No wonder that the clean-shaven boys of the past are anxious to assert themselves as men.

Beards may also be a reaction to the fact that gender roles are not so clearly demarcated today. When women continue to take over male roles in the workforce, and men are increasingly taking over domestic and familial roles, being stay-at-home dads, one way to establish male identity is to do it physically. And beards require no exercise.

The most striking aspect of beard behaviour is that it seems to be primarily aimed at other men. There is the famous photograph, for example, of Freud with his followers in the Vienna Circle standing out distinctly in the centre of the group, accentuated by his prominent beard, a hallmark of phallic power.

In a recent survey conducted by Lynx on people's attitudes to beards, sixty-three per cent of the men claimed that they thought they made men appear more manly and attractive, while ninety-two per cent of women preferred men without beards, and ninety-five per cent of women found men with stubble a turn-off. Men with beards may be having more fun, but it's not with women.

21 October 2009

33

Radovan Karadžić: all the signs of a psychopath

Like Goering, he also relished attention

In 1990, Radovan Karadžić said: "We don't want a single tear of a single child shed over the new state organisation, let alone a drop of blood." Today, nineteen years later, the "Beast of Bosnia" goes on trial at the International Criminal Tribunal for the Former Yugoslavia accused of genocide and war crimes. Not only did Karadžić's declaration of peaceful intent prove to be false, it heralded a future of lies and deception that could only be the work of a psychopath.

Dr Karadžić, founder of the Serbian Democratic Party, was indicted fourteen years ago and went into hiding for over a decade. He was arrested on 21 July 2008 on a bus in Belgrade, disguised by a thick beard and glasses. He had been posing as a doctor of alternative medicine under the name Dr Dragan David Dabić.

Now, aged sixty-four, Karadžić is charged with the massacre in 1995 of more than eight thousand Muslim men and boys at Sbrebrenica, the worst atrocity in Europe since the Second World War. He is also charged with organising the siege of Sarajevo, during which at least ten thousand people died in the sniping and shelling of the Bosnian capital by Bosnian Serb forces, and of masterminding the widespread use of torture and sexual abuse on prisoners of war.

It will be interesting to witness Karadžić's performance in court because he is a master showman and convincing conman. While the trial is expected to run for three years, Karadžić has been busy trying to buy time, partly, it is assumed, as a way of continuing to enjoy the relative comfort of the remand facilities of the court before the prospect of life imprisonment. His appeal for an extension of up to ten months to allow further time to prepare his defence was rejected by the court last week.

Karadžić left his birthplace, Montenegro, in 1960 to study medicine in Sarajevo. He was fifteen and described as convivial with a wide circle of friends drawn from the various ethnic groups in the city—Serbs, Croats, and Muslims. He was also described as slightly shady—living on credit at the local shops and playing poker for small stakes, paying his way through medical school.

He was raised by his mother in a small mountain village, while his father, a member of the Chetniks, was imprisoned by the post-war Communist regime for most of Karadžić's boyhood. It is possible that his father's long years of imprisonment may have fuelled Karadžić's ambition. In a poem, written in 1971 and dedicated to his father, Karadžić wrote, "Let's go down to the town and kill some scum". There was clearly some delinquent alliance with his father that Karadžić fostered in his mind.

Karadžić's intelligence and ability to win people over were considerable factors in his soaring career. From Sarajevo, he studied as a postgraduate, first in Denmark, and then in 1975 for a year at Columbia University in New York. He published his first work of poetry at the age of twenty-three and later married a wealthy fellow psychiatrist, Ljilijana Zelen, whose family undoubtedly helped him to become established.

Karadžić was known to falsify documents for his patients in return for bribes in order to supplement his income—a common practice among some professionals under the Yugoslav Socialist government. Karadžić's shady dealings first came to light when, working as a psychiatrist, he was accused in 1984 of embezzling money from his Belgrade hospital to build a ski chalet in Pale, a Bosnian village thirty kilometres east of Sarajevo. He served eleven months of a three-year sentence.

People who knew Karadžić during this time claim that it was his experience in prison and the power he obtained from his wife's money that changed him. After his release from jail, Karadžić took on a new image, wearing designer suits and taking up with members of the secret police and the underworld. His political views, previously with no allegiance to any particular ideology, became markedly Serbian nationalist. The groundwork was being laid for Karadžić's entry into the political arena.

It was the Serb nationalist author Dobrica Ćosić, later to become President of Yugoslavia, who recommended that the Serbian president Slobodan Milošević—the last high-profile Serb nationalist to stand trial at The Hague—appoint Karadžić as the leader of the Serbian Democratic Party.

In an interview following his appointment, Karadžić gave the disingenuous reply, "Everyone in Yugoslavia knows that I have never had any ambition to become a political leader. Every other politician refused to represent the party. It was too dangerous. I hoped that after the elections I would be free of any political function, but that was not possible ... They [the Croats] were preparing to kill us, to kill our people. The decision had to be made to organise the army."

In exaggerating the threat posed by opponents to the SDS, Karadžić presented himself as a reluctant hero who stepped into the breach in order to rescue the Serbian nationalists from extermination. As we now know, this was Karadžić's projection onto his opponents of his own intention to exterminate them.

It is ironic that Karadžić claims he was granted political immunity by Richard Holbrooke, the former US Assistant Secretary of State responsible for negotiating the 1995 Dayton Accord that ended the war in Bosnia. Holbrooke denies this and describes Karadžić as "the primary intellectual architect of the ethnic cleansing".

However, unlike Hitler, who instigated ethnic cleansing as part of a highly developed political ideology, Karadžić's ethnic cleansing was not founded on such evolved principles and seemed to be derived more directly from his own megalomania. Ideology was used by Karadžić as a rationale to dress up what was effectively thuggery.

What is especially chilling about Karadžić's performance throughout the Bosnian war is the outright lies he told and the way in which he revelled in the increasing attention he received from the international political community. In 1992, at the start of the siege on Sarajevo, Karadžić asserted, "We don't have a single sniper in Sarajevo ... Only the Muslims use snipers."

As Karadžić's power grew, he was invited to London and Switzerland for peace talks. Lord Owen, who had mediated in the Balkans, wrote of Karadžić, "At times I fell into the trap of underestimating Karadžić ... [He was] better than any other Serb except Milošević at negotiating, usually keeping cool, knowing when to give ground to protect vital interests and on occasion producing imaginative solutions." Karadžić won praise from his diplomatic colleagues for arguing the fine points of agreements—agreements he had no intention of fulfilling. His ability to con people was never more evident.

Karadžić enjoyed flaunting his power publicly. In 1994, he invited a guest from Russia, the ultra-nationalist poet Eduard

Limonov, to the front lines in order to fire a few anti-aircraft rounds on the populace of Sarajevo. Limonov fired without hesitation and the entire episode was televised.

Another television moment showed Karadžić playing chess with his military commander Ratko Mladić with the racket of 50,000 Muslims being shelled in the background. It is Karadžić's explicit pleasure in advertising these acts that so strongly suggests the mentality of a psychopath.

Journalists who have seen Karadžić at The Hague comment on his charisma. He is about to receive the greatest attention he will ever win from the world. Perhaps this is what Karadžić has sought, through his criminal acts, all along?

There is a haunting parallel with Hermann Goering's performance at the Nuremberg trials. Richard Sonnenfeldt, the chief US translater, whose obituary appeared in the *Times* last Thursday, singled out Goering as charming and slippery. Goering seemed to relish the attention he received at the trial. There was no recognition of the horror of his actions or of their impact on others. On the contrary, the trial was an opportunity to publicise and defend his achievements.

Goering, it seems, did not fall into Hannah Arendt's category of the "banality of evil" that is committed by ordinary people. Instead, we see the psychopath who cannot differentiate between right and wrong, who is incapable of concern and guilt, and whose primary aim is to feel powerful, instilling awe and terror in others. Their triumph is to con people into believing they are "normal".

Karadžić's training in psychiatry would have helped him to develop this persona and to place him firmly on the other side of madness.

EDITOR'S NOTE: After this item was posted, Radovan Karadžić yesterday failed to turn up for his trial, saying he needed at least another nine months to prepare his defence. The hearing was then adjourned. However, today the judge said the trial could go ahead in Karadžić's absence, explaining that he must face the consequences of his decision to stay away.

27 October 2009

34

You're the one! Dangers of internet dating

This week's rape report proves the net is a breeding ground for unrealistic sexual fantasies

A young woman of twenty-three met "Derek" several times before inviting him back to her house. They had first "met" on an internet dating site. On 30 September, they arranged to meet on the M2 where he followed her car back to her block of flats in south London.

The woman was with her three-year-old son, and while they were having tea together, "Derek" punched the woman unconscious and then raped her in front of her son. *According to yesterday's reports*, she and her son later escaped and fled to the police.

Internet dating sites are careful to warn their clients about the need to meet in public places, at least initially, and not to give out personal details, such as last names or addresses, before getting to know someone. The snag comes when getting to know someone, particularly a stranger, is not so clear cut.

While there are countless stories of happily married couples who met on the internet, there are even more stories ranging from the ludicrous to the dangerous. What many of these stories demonstrate is that internet dating is a prolific breeding ground for romantic and sexual fantasies that may have little to do with reality.

A middle-aged man rushes into a hotel bar where he is meeting "Dance Ticket". He is over an hour late and has telephoned "Dance Ticket" to explain he has been caught in traffic: can she just hold on? She waits and wonders how typical this is, but his profile and their conversation on the phone the previous week seemed promising.

Then he appears, throws his coat over a chair, orders a glass of wine for himself. "Dance Ticket" is already on her second and, as his eyes flit to the other people talking in the bar, declares, "You're perfect! I knew it: you're the one for me!"

The *idée fixe* of the perfect partner is fraught with problems and usually indicates someone who has idealised a parental figure and who is blindly and impulsively looking for a similar match. But the idealisation often covers up underlying conflicts that can't be acknowledged, including, at its most extreme, hatred.

We all have templates of our parents in our minds as our first love objects. But these templates tend to become fixed in our fantasies when there have been difficulties and traumas. When this happens, the child in the mind of the adult continues to search for a parent whose love may have been mixed with either ill-treatment or with certain expectations of how they wanted their child to be. This way of being loved is then repeated in future relationships, what Freud coined the "repetition compulsion", and inevitably leads to heartache. For internet entrepreneurs, this is the perfect customer because they can be sure they will return for more.

All internet daters have an agenda of some kind. Some internet daters are only looking for a sexual partner. They either freely admit they have no interest in any other form of relationship or they say they do when they don't. But these daters also have particular fantasies that they are hoping to fulfil, even if the fantasies entail being rejected or rejecting others. And sometimes, as in the case of "Derek", the fantasies are much more violent.

The internet provides the perfect *tabula rasa* for daters to search for their fantasy partner and to enact the powerful and often damaging relationships of their past. Although romantic illusion does not only exist in cyberspace, the internet feeds people's desire for instant relationships and instant solutions and an instant fix. The net effect is that there is increasing pressure amongst the dating culture to be able to find "the one" for you by a few simple trawls through profiles intended to promote various fantasy scenarios.

The real danger in internet dating is that it encourages the ideal of the perfect match and reduces the complex business of building a relationship into a shopping exercise. Dating is the new commodity with trial periods, exchanges, and returns offered—but no refunds. Buyer beware!

9 November 2009

35

Is Khmer Rouge jailer Duch just a nobody?

Watching Duch give evidence is reminiscent of Eichmann

Comrade Duch, now a born-again Christian lay preacher, admitted to the Cambodian missionary responsible for his conversion, Christopher LaPel, that he "did a lot of bad things in his life", deeds for which he was not sure he could be forgiven.

Comrade Duch (pronounced *Doik*) has been on trial in Cambodia since February 2009 for supervising the torture and killings of some 16,000 men, women, and children at the notorious Khmer Rouge prison known as S-21 between 1975 and 1979.

Today, at the end of the hearings, the prosecution called for a "lengthy jail term" following evidence that Duch was guilty of war crimes and crimes against humanity.

A devoted member of the Khmer Rouge, Duch's defence is that he was following orders from higher-ups in the regime and it would have been fatal to disobey.

Watching clips of Duch's testimony in court, what is so chilling is that this sixty-six-year-old former maths teacher, who was responsible for atrocities on such a massive scale, appears to be so ordinary. A wiry man, with a lined face and crooked teeth, Duch joins the ranks of "ordinary" men who in the last century were the conduits for mass exterminations under orders from oppressive political regimes.

The judges conducting the Khmer Rouge trials have limited the prosecution to the four most senior surviving party members in addition to Kaing Guek Eav, aka Comrade Duch, who is the least senior officer on trial.

His testimony has been chosen first because, out of the five, he is the only one to admit responsibility for his actions and the only one to express remorse and to cooperate with the prosecution. The four more senior officers claim that their subordinates carried out the killings without their knowledge and out of over-zealous loyalty to the party.

There are striking parallels with the Khmer Rouge trials and Eichmann's trial in Jerusalem in 1961. Hugh Trevor-Roper in the *Times* compared the experience of witnessing Eichmann's trial to the Nuremberg trials, describing it as "a trial for shrunken puppets hiding behind a master who had disappeared".

Hannah Arendt, in her groundbreaking work *Eichmann in Jerusalem: A Report on the Banality of Evil*, published in 1961, argued that Eichmann, along with countless other Nazis and Nazi sympathisers, was not motivated to commit the atrocities of the Nazi regime through hatred and malevolence but rather through lack of thought, imagination, and memory. These are the basic ingredients found in what Arendt describes as the "nobodies" who commit evil. Just as Eichmann was described as a loving family man, there are similarly stories of Duch's kindness and his sense of humour.

We tend to want to categorise people who commit evil deeds as either "bad" or "mad". This way, we can feel that evil-doers are "other" than us, and we can disassociate ourselves from them. The trouble with Eichmann and now Duch is that they are neither "bad" nor "mad", and it is just their ordinariness that makes their deeds so very disturbing. They challenge our belief that we would act differently in their place.

Arendt writes: "In granting pardon, it is the person and not the crime that is forgiven; in rootless evil there is no person left whom one could ever forgive." She introduces the idea that neither remorse nor guilt can be experienced by the sort of "nobody" who has chosen to follow orders within a regime and has abnegated his thinking entirely to a higher authority. Remorse and guilt rely on some degree of self-reflection and an inner dialogue that allows for the questioning and assessment of one's actions in relation to others as well as the act of remembering what has been done. Arendt thought that the reason Eichmann was able to oversee such atrocities was because he lacked the imagination to understand emotionally the consequences of his actions and to empathise with his victims' suffering. This is only possible when there is no self-reflection or inner dialogue—when a person is in reality a "nobody" not a "somebody".

In his preliminary hearing last February, Duch emphasised the blind loyalty that was required in Pol Pot's regime, to the point that its members would not flinch at denouncing their relatives and closest loved ones. Duch justified the tortures he conducted and ordered on the basis of his devotion to the revolution and its cause. Torture was also the best means of eliciting confessions and unearthing subversives who would undermine the regime.

This is horribly reminiscent of US policy on the torture of prisoners in Guantanamo Bay and Abu Ghraib. "When we have rid our country of the vermin that infect people's minds," Duch explained, "when we have liberated it from this army of cowards and traitors who debase the people, then we will rebuild a Cambodia of solidarity, united by genuine bonds of fraternity and equality."

Having justified torture as necessary for the protection of the regime, Duch later admitted that he "was, from an early time, sceptical of the veracity of the confessions", and that "even the Standing Committee, in my opinion, did not really believe in it".

It is clear that the torture and subsequent killing of all the prisoners were exercises intended "to eliminate those who represented obstacles". In addition to this, it was an effective way of controlling party members through fear.

Co-prosecutor Chea Leang argues that Duch was "indifferent to the suffering of the victims" at S-21. As the key intelligence operative of the Khmer Rouge, Duch was, in Leang's words, "the trusted man to identify supposed plots against the revolution and to root out enemies".

In his defence, Duch claims that he had no choice but to comply with the cruelties of the regime within which he operated: "When I was forced to supervise (the prison), I became both an actor in criminal acts and also a hostage of the regime." The indictment concluded that Duch was "paralysed by fear for his life, wondering when it would be his turn".

While Duch accepts his responsibility for what he did, his testimony raises the question as to how any of us would behave under such a regime? If one is trapped within a regime that itself is primarily committed to establishing total power and lacks imagination and a space for self-reflection, is it possible to remain a "somebody"?

When a person is treated as a "nobody", which can happen even within the regime of a tyrannical family, then behaving as a "nobody"—wiping out any internal thought processes that might question what is going on—may be the only way to survive.

24 November 2009

On 2 February 2012, Kaing Guek Eav, known as Comrade Duch, was sentenced to life imprisonment by the Extraordinary Chambers in the Courts of Cambodia.

36

Why some women bosses turn into bullies

The guiding mantra for Mrs Glenda Stone, the woman who until recently headed a government task force to assist women in business, was "profit before passion". She is known for criticising women who are not driven by the desire to make money, describing their business ventures as "charities or hobbies".

Earlier this week, she was ordered by the Central London Employment Tribunal to pay more than £28,000 in compensation to the employees, men and women, who had accused her of bullying them.

Stone, a straight-talking Australian of forty-two, was appointed co-chair of the Women's Enterprise Task Force in November 2006. She had a strong track record of supporting women in business. In 2000, she set up Aurora, a women's networking, recruitment, and events firm. She also founded the annual Where Women Want to Work Top 50.

In many respects, she was the obvious and ideal candidate for the job. But her recent indictment by the tribunal tells another story.

The stereotype of the woman boss who is tougher than any of the guys around—and awful to work for—is, despite feminism, still alive and well. Many women entering business think that the way to succeed is to out-man their male colleagues.

The classic example is the phallic portrayal of Miranda Priestly, the fashion magazine editor modelled on *Vogue*'s Anna Wintour, in the film *The Devil Wears Prada*. Her ultra-feminine appearance and obsequious deference to those above her thinly mask the contempt she exudes for everyone beneath her and her vicious competitiveness.

Behind the scenes, the story that has unfolded about Mrs Stone reveals a similar ruthless bully. She has been accused by three former employees of being "controlling", "inflexible", "dictatorial", and "intimidating". When they complained about her bullying, they were fired within days.

Her former personal assistant, Janette King, told the tribunal, "I developed a nervous twitch, which I did not have before and which stopped as soon as I stopped working there." Mrs King was dismissed by email after she confronted Mrs Stone about her bullying behaviour.

Another former employee, David Collier, who had worked for Aurora for two-and-a-half years, was threatened with a salary cut of nearly forty per cent following a row. The next day, he received a letter of redundancy for "financial reasons". Stone denied these claims, but the tribunal chairman said his panel had been "unimpressed" by some of her evidence.

Stone has made it very clear that the only worthwhile goal of running a business is to make a profit. "Passion", feelings, and concern for others in the form of social responsibility are eschewed by her as being the downfall of women in business.

She argues that: "For some reason, women want to be the Zeitgeist. They want to create something that did not exist before. They want to do something that they find emotionally and psychologically rewarding." Her denigration of what women want betrays her low opinion of herself as a woman, and above all her fear of feelings. This could be one reason why Mrs Stone holds her female employees in such contempt.

On the other hand, male employees are often even greater targets for women bosses who bully. Stone, like Miranda Priestly and other women bully bosses, worships the phallic god of money. This is the male world of power in which they want to succeed. It is also a world, at least in the fantasy of the woman boss, impervious to feeling and therefore providing an illusion of control and security. These women's desire to be top "man" in a man's world and bullying their way into this position belies their envy of men and what they represent to them.

This is what Freud called "penis envy". When envious feelings are too painful to acknowledge, the ego defends itself by either adopting an attitude of superiority over others—there is no one to be envious of because I have it all and they are the inadequate ones—or inferiority—in comparison with others, I am no good because I don't have what someone else has.

When a woman has been made to feel ashamed of herself and her feelings, for whatever reason, she is more likely to be envious of men. She defends herself from knowing about this by adopting a position of supremacy over both men and women, while at the same time she denigrates herself in her mind. The result is that the more divorced she feels from her feelings, the worse she feels about herself and the more she is likely to go on the attack.

A recent example of this was a London media boss who regularly called the senior men under her command "cunts". Any woman who swears like this not only hates men but she hates herself. The castration is ultimately directed against her own feelings.

There are numerous examples of women who are in top positions in business in this country and abroad who have achieved success because they have combined both masculine and feminine qualities in their approach to work.

Many successful women view their feelings as a guide to inform their thinking and decision-making rather than a hindrance to success. They have not had to become "men" to succeed. The women bosses who bully and show contempt for their feelings and those of others do not promote women in business, they promote a phallocentric marketplace in which both men and women suffer.

4 December 2009

37

What deniers of climate change are really denying

**Griffin, Palin, and others show the sort of
narcissism seen in small children**

In a speech in the European parliament last month, Nick Griffin, leader of the ultra-right British National Party, referred to the scientists and politicians who are urging international controls to curb the effects of climate change as "cranks". Griffin, who is now one of the MEPs representing the European Union at Copenhagen, went on to state that "an Orwellian consensus" had been reached, "based not on scientific agreement, but on bullying censorship and fraudulent statistics".

What Griffin claims is almost exactly the opposite of the truth. While there is overwhelming scientific evidence that climate change is happening and that we are actively influencing it for the worse, there is no scientific agreement to the contrary. The bullying censorship he refers to has taken place in the lab break-ins and computer hacking used to acquire selective evidence, which is then taken out of context to support the deniers' argument.

In short, Griffin and his followers are vilifying their opponents by tarnishing them with what is in effect their own desire to distort the truth in order to support their own political agenda.

The supporters of climate change are now also tagged as the "new Reds". In the same speech, Griffin said: "The anti-Western intellectual cranks of the left suffered a collective breakdown when communism collapsed. Climate change is their new theology ... But the heretics will have a voice in Copenhagen and the truth will out. Climate change is being used to impose an anti-human utopia as deadly as anything conceived by Stalin or Mao."

This is the rhetoric of the Cold War. The "anti-Western intellectual cranks" need to be eradicated and the purity of the Western state preserved. Not surprisingly, this accords with Griffin's hardline anti-immigration policy. The threat to self-preservation is seen to be coming from the "intellectuals" who want, in the minds of Griffin and others, to establish a totalitarian state that has complete control over the individual.

Control is the key issue for the deniers of climate change—control over the way we live and how we use the world's resources. Sarah Palin, another denier of the evidence for climate change, has ironically called for better scientific evidence: evidence that she hopes will counter the findings that we have now and demonstrate that the restrictions being urged on our use of energy are merely a means of political control rather than based on any reality of damage limitation.

Palin, like other politicians who deny climate change, is anxious because she sees the debate about climate change as not only having global implications but as conferring power over the future of our lives. And she is right.

Climate change threatens our narcissistic omnipotence. Deniers do not want anyone else telling them they can't drive large cars or run two refrigerators. They want to hold on to the belief that not only does Mother Earth have unlimited resources but that these resources should remain entirely within their control.

This is a mentality resembling the narcissism of small children who want to hold on to their illusion of omnipotence and control over mother. Any threat to their position is experienced as a narcissistic wound that is tolerable only to the extent that their attachment to mother is relatively secure.

This is part of normal early development that we all go through. Narcissism at this stage is a necessary defence against the actual vulnerability of the infant that could otherwise be overwhelming. It also serves to protect the child from anxiety about separation and loss. In our minds, it is a state of being-at-one with mother and the world. As we grow up, the limitations of reality inevitably challenge our omnipotence and we learn how to accept external restrictions along with our own vulnerability and ultimate death.

The deniers of climate change represent a part of our world psyche that is desperately trying to maintain the narcissistic illusion that we can continue to plunder the world's resources without any consequences: in other words, that mother's breast is there for the taking.

However, as the world breast begins to dry up, the anxiety about loss, vulnerability, and our own destructiveness becomes increasingly hard to bear. One way to control anxiety is to deny reality. Reality itself becomes the enemy that challenges this narcissistic hegemony and must be attacked accordingly. The need to maintain control then turns into paranoia.

While scientists are being accused of conspiring to distort the truth in order to wrest control over others, this is precisely what the deniers of climate change are doing.

17 December 2009

38

Jessica Davies' heady cocktail of sex and pain

Why pick up a stranger and stab him to death?

Jessica Davies, thirty-year-old niece of Britain's junior defence minister Quentin Davies, was sentenced this week to fifteen years in jail for *fatally stabbing Olivier Mugnier*, a twenty-four-year-old unemployed graduate nicknamed "Funtime", whom she picked up at an Irish pub in Paris for a night of drugs and sex on 11 November 2007. When she realised what she had done, she telephoned emergency services and was found covered in blood, cradling Mugnier's dead body. She told police, "It's me who did it. I don't know why, but I did it … I am a monster."

During her trial in Versailles, Davies made no attempt to deny the murder but told the jury that she had no memory of her attack except "the sensation of the knife going in".

The story unfolded that after inviting Mugnier back to her flat, they tried to have sex but were unable to do so because of the drugs and alcohol they had both consumed. Davies then took a knife from her kitchen and, while Mugnier was sitting naked on her bed, she thought of cutting him but lost control. "I just wanted to cut him a little, but (the blade) went in by itself", she explained to the court. Mugnier suffered multiple stab wounds to his throat and upper body.

While experts told the court that Davies' consumption of alcohol, various anti-depressant pills, and cannabis would have made her aggressive, this is only a partial explanation of her behaviour.

In court, Monique Henry, Davies' mother, described her daughter as "an adolescent who was disturbed by family difficulties" and who was, as an adult, "unable to face day-to-day life".

Davies was clearly depressed. She had split up with her boyfriend of four years, she had failed at her modelling career, she "mechanically changed friends every year", she was unable to control her drinking, and prior to Mugnier's death, she had started cutting her arms and legs and had attempted suicide with the same knife she used in her attack on Mugnier.

Davies was also described as having had a troubled and dysfunctional childhood. Her mother seems to attribute much of her daughter's distress to the fact that her father had been absent through much of her childhood, eventually leaving the family to live abroad with his mistress.

However, Davies' symptoms suggest that she may well have a personality disorder, as her defence argued, that has its roots in infancy and difficulties in her primary relationship with her mother. Davies, on her own admission, confessed, "I don't know how to bond with other people".

Cutting indicates a serious disturbance and is usually associated with extreme alienation and dissociation of feelings. Cutting and feeling pain is a way of confirming that the person exists in the world. The pain, even though it is self-inflicted, alleviates the stress of being alone. The pain becomes linked with the pleasure of existing and provides an illusion of love as well as a necessary discharge of anxiety.

The profound insecurity that is evident in this form of self-destructive behaviour invariably points to a relationship between the mother and infant that is inconsistent and experienced as unbearably painful by the infant.

This may happen, for example, if a mother is unable to understand or respond to her baby's emotions to such an extent that the baby is left having to manage overwhelming feelings of anger, distress, and fear on her own. For a baby, this can be equivalent to what we can imagine as being left in the middle of the ocean at the mercy of the elements.

In order to survive this early trauma, the baby begins to take refuge in physical sensations of pain that not only provide a kind of life raft but are a channel for the baby's angry and aggressive feelings that are also overwhelming.

The traumatised baby will direct anger against herself in order to ensure that she does not destroy or damage the mother. In the baby's mind, her mother's emotional unavailability has been caused by her, and this creates a powerful sense of unconscious guilt and badness in the baby. As Davies declared when she lost control and killed Mugnier, "I am a monster".

But how does this painful enactment, stemming from infancy, become linked to sexual excitement?

A complex scenario is established in the baby's mind with its love object. In order to deny an awareness of the pain that the baby experiences from her mother, the anger and frustration is turned into something exciting and stimulating. In later life, this excitement is expressed sexually and this early scenario is played out in sexual relationships. Love is confused with hate, and suffering becomes a way of holding onto the love object. Better to be in pain with someone than to have no one there at all.

We know very little about Davies' relationships with men, except that in the case of Mugnier she picked him up with the intention of having sex. What is interesting is that when he proved to be impotent, Davies' mind turned to cutting him. Being unable to get rid of her emotional pain and anger through sex, she may well have found herself—in her mind—back with a mother who failed to respond to her.

In her heightened state of aggression, this failure may have been the last straw for Davies. The aggression that she had previously directed against herself—her cutting and her suicide attempts—came out against Mugnier.

Unfortunately for Mugnier, it is very likely that he was playing the part of Davies' mother—the mother towards whom she felt so murderous. When Davies cut Mugnier, instead of herself, she exposed the real monster in her mind.

14 January 2010

39

Edlington brothers: why boredom turns to torture

How could two young boys be so sadistic? The dangers of having "nowt to do"

Two brothers, aged ten and eleven, lure two other boys into empty wasteland near a playground on the pretext of seeing a dead fox. They then savagely attack the two boys, bludgeoning one of them unconscious, after torturing them both and sexually assaulting one of the boys. The brothers, showing no remorse for what they have done, explain they had "nowt to do".

This morning, the two brothers from the Edlington suburb of Doncaster were sentenced at Sheffield Crown Court to an indefinite period of detention. Mr Justice Keith called their behaviour "appalling and terrible" and said their detention must last a minimum of five years.

"The fact is, this was prolonged, sadistic violence for no reason other than that you got a real kick out of hurting and humiliating them", said the judge. "The bottom line for the two of you is that I'm sure you both pose a very high risk of serious harm to others."

What has been most shocking for those following the Sheffield court case has been that the brothers have shown no feeling for their victims. They admitted that they only stopped hitting their victims because their "arms were hurting".

These were not isolated attacks on the part of the brothers. A string of previous attacks on other children, vandalism, and violent behaviour in school had already brought the brothers to the attention of Doncaster social services and the police. While the brothers' behaviour and callousness indicate that they may both be psychopathic, their "toxic" home environment suggests another explanation.

The older brother has described "routine aggression, violence, and chaos" at home. The father, a heavy drinker, physically abused their mother, threatening in front of the boys to "take a knife to her and slice her face to bits". When the boys, or any of their five brothers, tried to intervene to stop the father's attacks on their mother, their father would turn on them.

On the other hand, the boys seem to have been allowed in many respects to do as they pleased, watching horror movies that were particularly gruesome and having access to their father's pornographic DVDs.

The boys' mother has been described as passively suffering at the hands of her husband and sitting at home most of the time doing nothing. A neighbour has also said that she witnessed the mother putting cannabis in the boys' food in order to keep them calm and get them to sleep. Perhaps this was the mother's attempt to medicate her children and herself, as a way of not only controlling the boys' aggression but anaesthetising them against the pain and violence they were all subjected to.

In the midst of this extreme neglect and violence, what is also striking is the boys' explanation that they attacked their victims because there was "nowt to do". They were bored and looking for excitement.

"Being bored" is complex and can often mask deeper feelings of anxiety, dread, and depression. The boys had witnessed their mother sitting at home with nothing to do and may well have feared becoming mindless and depressed like her.

While the mother may have turned her aggression against herself in a masochistic way, the boys enacted their sadism against others, often in imitation of their father's behaviour. The older boy was known to have punched and kicked two teachers and to have punched a mother with small children on the street. The younger brother also hit one teacher and head-butted another.

For the two brothers, not having anything to do may have faced them with a space in which they had to experience their thoughts and feelings about their relationships and what was happening to them. When there has been no parent to acknowledge or understand these feelings, they are experienced as unbearable and must be expelled in whatever way possible. Otherwise, the child faces the terrible fear of becoming psychotic.

As a way of managing the trauma of their lives, the boys may have had to cut off from their own feelings, including their concern for others, and seek relief from their anxiety about their murderous feelings towards their parents by directing their aggression against other adults and children.

In the case of the attacks on other children, it was also a way for the boys to inflict the torture that they had suffered at home on other children. In this way, they could triumph mentally by becoming the torturer and negating their own helplessness as victims.

There seems to have been no parental limit set on either the violence committed at home or the violent behaviour of the boys. As a result, we can see the boys engaged in a trajectory of increasingly violent "things to do".

This may have been an unconscious cry for help, a test to see who would finally stop them, but it also shows an escalation that is very common in perverse forms of behaviour. The violent behaviour only relieves pent-up aggression momentarily and is usually accompanied by guilt, which in turn requires punishment, and this leads to a further and more intense cycle of violence.

Having "nowt to do" can be a dangerous thing.

22 January 2010

40

Pope John Paul II: saint or closet masochist?

The late Pope may have been searching for love and a release from guilt

Pope Benedict XVI has put John Paul II on the fast track to sainthood, waiving the customary five-year waiting period, following John Paul II's death in April 2005. And as *The First Post* reported this week, Monsignor Slavomir Oder, the Vatican's chief promoter of his sainthood, has published a book, *Why He Is a Saint: The Real John Paul II*, which enumerates his various saintly practices. Self-mortification is high on the list.

Penitence is meant to bring the worshipper closer to God. For John Paul, this took the form of sleeping on a hard floor instead of his bed, starving during Lent, and flagellating himself with a special belt that he kept in his closet amongst his vestments.

There is no doubt that John Paul regarded beating himself as a reminder of the suffering of Jesus on the cross. Oder explains: "It should be seen as part of his profound relationship with the Lord." Indeed, self-mortification is a necessary criterion for sainthood and has been a fundamental aspect of Christianity since its beginnings.

But where is the line drawn between saintliness and masochism, or are they flip-sides of the same coin?

While Catholicism teaches that the human body is a gift from God, denial of basic needs and bodily comfort is also encouraged as a form of resistance to venal desires. This is, of course, not exclusive to Catholicism. Most religions promote some form of self-sacrifice. Sacrifice can help people endure deprivation on earth with the promise of rewards in heaven.

It is also true that the spiritual need to submit to a higher authority and to relinquish individual needs in order to gain a sense of communion with the world is something intrinsically human. In psychological terms, it can be understood as our desire to return to the womb, to be completely at one with mother, and to eradicate any conflict and loss brought about by separateness.

However, penitence goes a step further and entails not simply sacrifice but punishment as well. The more pain is inflicted, the greater love is shown to God, and the more God loves his follower. Guilt is at the heart of penitence.

There is a striking parallel here to the way in which children who have had depressed parents or who have lost their parents through death or separation often respond by blaming themselves and seek punishment in the hope of restoring the lost object.

By assuming responsibility for the disasters that occur in the family, the child maintains some illusion of control in a world of chaos and unpredictability. The child is then in the grip of an unconscious guilt that can become persecuting and can have destructive consequences in later life.

In order to feel loved once again, the child tries to be especially "good". This often means that the child—and later the adult—punishes himself for having needs and desires that he attributes as being the root cause of the disaster. Selfishness is the sin that must be punished.

John Paul was careful to keep his self-mortification private. Although he often slept on the floor, he messed up his bed sheets to disguise the fact. His private acts of penitence can be seen as his attempt to expiate the sins of others, following Jesus. They may also suggest that he was searching for love and a release from guilt through his own self-inflicted suffering.

John Paul was a young adult during the Nazi occupation of Poland and must have witnessed overwhelming suffering, especially amongst the Jewish community with whom he had grown up in his home town of Wadowice.

He also experienced terrible losses within his own family. His older sister had died in infancy before his birth, and it is certainly possible that he had to cope with a depressed mother in his early infancy. After his mother died when he was eight, he became close to his brother, fourteen years older, who in his practice as a doctor contracted scarlet fever and subsequently died. His father, a non-commissioned army officer, later died of a heart attack. By the time he was twenty, John Paul said, "I had already lost all the people I loved."

Beating himself may have been one way in which John Paul was able to keep his relationship with the members of his family alive and to fend off the losses that were beyond his control. On the spiritual side of the coin, John Paul was keeping alive his relationship with Jesus and with God.

29 January 2010

41

Sports stars lose out to philanthropists as today's heroes

With the sudden fall of the now former England captain, John Terry, following hard on the heels of Tiger Woods' dented career, sports stars are no longer the role models they used to be. Their successes don't seem to make them better people but reveal instead their arrogance and insecurity.

To rate as a role model, the person must represent something of our higher nature. Sports stars, going back to the inception of the Olympics in ancient Greece, have long been acclaimed as heroes whose superhuman achievements demonstrate that man can rise to the level of the gods, even if only for a moment. These are the stars who set the standard we aspire to.

Our role models do not normally have affairs, or give in to lust, greed, or avarice—at least not publicly. They embody qualities that we admire. Like the loved father and mother of our childhood, they shape our ideal of who we want to be when we grow up. Having an ideal serves a vital component in our psychological development and in our psychic health. Striving towards our ideal helps us to bear frustration, to sublimate instinctual gratification, so that we can think, learn, and develop the necessary skills to be creative. Without a desire to be like his father, the little boy would never leave the comfort of his mother's arms.

The recent disillusionment with sports stars coincides with the effects of the recession and our changing images of success. The successful banker, waving at us from his yacht in the south of France, the gawping star created by reality TV, and the bejewelled supermodel are only a few of the role models that seem to have died out as money is scarce and the narcissistic goals of fame and power are considerably harder to achieve.

So who are the role models we look up to now?

Disasters often bring out the best in people and also afford an opportunity for new role models to emerge. The crisis in Haiti has, for example, provoked an overwhelming philanthropic response, much of it led noticeably by Hollywood stars. George Clooney, Simon Cowell, and Sean Penn have perhaps achieved most recognition, but there are scores of other actors and media stars who are also rushing in to provide relief. The men tend to bring in money and immediate emergency aid. Clooney and Cowell are raising money. Tom Cruise and John Travolta are flying in the Scientologists to provide aid and spiritual support. Meanwhile, the women tend to be more concerned with the care of the elderly and children. Madonna and Angelina Jolie express their philanthropy by adopting children.

As we become increasingly aware of our dwindling resources, the goal of acquisition is gradually being replaced with that of giving. Making large sums of money—the banker's bonus and the footballer's salary—is now largely regarded with opprobrium. Making money for the benefit of others is the new criterion of success.

The great philanthropists of the last century, such as Carnegie, Rowntree, Rockefeller, Ford, and more recently, Gates, Soros, and Buffett, made their fortunes primarily in finance and industry.

While these men may be role models for some of us, the media star is by and large someone with whom we can identify more easily and who is a more accessible role model. The media star also conveys another message.

The new philanthropist is more powerful than the role model of the sports star because he is someone who has converted his narcissism into altruism. The incentive to perform well and to achieve recognition are still there, but are now coupled with the power attached to giving to others.

Narcissistic gratification is achieved through an act of selflessness. Whereas the sports star has to overcome his selfish drives through the discipline of training and adherence to the rules of the game, the philanthropist gives others' needs priority over his own. Real success is not simply being good at what one does or winning the competition, it entails having a heart. The new alpha male is the most successful giver.

While the philanthropist presents us with a noble aspiration, it is not without its shadow. On one side is the gentle face of power that brings us close to the beneficence of the gods. And on the other side is the darker face of self-interest. To be effective, a role model must be genuine. Beware the fakes.

7 February 2010

42

Tokyo: when a "splitter-upper" goes too far

Hired by a husband to seduce his wife, Takeshi Kuwabara made the mistake of falling in love …

Prosecutors in Tokyo called this week for Takeshi Kuwabara to be given a seventeen-year jail sentence for the murder of his lover, Rie Ishohata. This was no ordinary love affair gone wrong. Kuwabara had been hired by Rie's husband to seduce her in order to obtain grounds for divorce. In short, Kuwabara was what the Japanese call a "splitter-upper". He made the fatal mistake of falling in love with his client's wife.

Kuwabara worked for one of the *wakaresaseya*—meaning "splitter-upper"—agencies that have multiplied in Japan over the past few years. The agents are basically private detectives who go a step further than your traditional gumshoe: they don't simply spy on their prey, they enter their lives in disguise in order to split up relationships. An initial consultation may cost 10,000 yen—about £70—and costs then escalate depending on the complexity of the case.

In the case of Kuwabara, he managed to engineer an encounter with thirty-two-year-old Rie as she was shopping in her local supermarket in a northern suburb of Tokyo. Calling himself Hajime, he innocently asked where he could find a shop that sold good cheesecake. They got to talking, one thing led to another, and they became lovers. The couple were eventually photographed entering a "love hotel", all arranged behind the scenes by Kuwabara himself.

But here's where it went wrong: by the time Kuwabara had accomplished his mission, he and Rie had fallen in love. "Hajime" did not disclose at the time that he had a wife and children. Only after two years did he reveal to Rie his part in her break-up with her husband. Shocked to learn the truth, she said she was leaving him—and, in his rage, he strangled her. When Kuwabara surrendered himself to the police, he said: "I still love her".

While this is an extreme case, it signals the dangers of *wakaresaseya*. The agencies offer their service not only to husbands and wives who want to get out of their marriages, but also to wives who want someone to seduce their husband's mistress so their husband will come back to them, to parents who want to break up a son or daughter's unsuitable relationship, and to employers who want to procure the resignation of an employee.

The agencies, which are unregulated, flourish because they help their clients keep face and avoid personal confrontation, both of which are important in Japanese culture.

However, what is most appealing about the *wakaresaseya* service is that it offers a relatively shame-free solution to relationship problems. The spouse or boss never has to admit that they are unhappy or feel hurt and vulnerable; nor do they need to admit any wrongdoing or failure. By hiring someone else to entice wives, husbands, and employees to err, they can come out as the injured party. How often have we fantasised about finding someone else to do our dirty work when we want to get out of a relationship?

Wakaresaseya is also successful because it enables clients to act out their forbidden fantasies and to have the illusion that they can behave like the gods who "toy with the emotions of human beings", as Rie Ishohata's grieving father remarked. The forsaken wife can get rid of her rival; parents can alter their child's lives; businessmen can force the hand of their colleagues—all with a simple phone call. There is an assumption not only that other people can be controlled but that it is acceptable, if not desirable, to do so. Shame is fundamentally equated with helplessness and an inability to be in control of one's own situation and that of others.

The ethics and legitimacy of these agencies are being questioned in Japan, especially in the wake of the Tokyo trial. Nevertheless, the agencies thrive because they offer a remedy that not only alleviates shame and but also allows clients to fulfil their deepest fantasies by proxy.

But what is it that motivates those who are employed as "splitter-uppers"?

They are often actors, models, or personable people looking for part-time work. They are employed to act out specific scenarios that also require a certain amount of imagination and ingenuity. But the real challenge is whether they can *destroy* a relationship— and this holds a certain excitement in itself. It is a pathway to Oedipal triumph that is not only encouraged but remunerative as well.

And herein lies the danger. Having broken up Rie's marriage and made her dependent on him, Kuwabara may have felt unconsciously that he had got rid of his "father" and regained his "mother" for himself. Like Oedipus and his mother Jocaste, they lived happily together until one day the truth came out and then all hell broke lose. Kuwabara's solution was to kill his lover rather than to face life without her and with the truth of what he had done.

Wakaresaseya promises clients an easy way out of their problems, but the reality is that it blinds both clients and agents to the destructiveness of their actions. Like the gods, the *wakaresaseya* agencies are left to laugh at the foibles of the mortals they exploit.

There are surely better ways of saying "*sayonara*"—goodbye.

12 February 2010

43

The biggest bully is inside Gordon Brown's head

Brown's fear of displeasing his father has driven him to make impossible demands of himself—and others

Gordon Brown, in a speech last April at St. Paul's Cathedral in London, espoused the Christian doctrine to "do to others what you would have them do unto you". These words strike an ironic chord in the midst of accusations of a "bullying culture" within 10 Downing Street. It might be closer to the truth to think that Gordon Brown is doing unto others what he does to himself.

In an interview with Channel 4, in which he sought to deal with the accusations of bullying and intimidation in Andrew Rawnsley's book *The End of the Party*, Gordon Brown denied he had once assaulted an aide. "I have never, never hit anybody in my life", he protested. "I don't do these sorts of things. I was brought up (by) my father (and) I never heard him say an unkind word about anyone. In the heat of the moment, you say things sometimes. You do get angry, mostly with yourself. But I'm strong-willed and I'm very determined ... Every morning I get up with a determination to do my best for this country."

The clue to Brown's outbursts is evident in his saying, "You do get angry, mostly with yourself." He also emphasises his strong will and determination. These are undoubtedly positive attributes, but they can also become destructive ones if they are pushed to an extreme. It seems clear that Brown is someone who has high expectations of himself—so high, in fact, that the result may be persecuting, both to himself and to others.

At an early age, it was clear that Brown was exceptionally bright in school and a high achiever. Brown is typical of many high achievers who push themselves relentlessly and often treat others in the same way, unaware of the harmful effect they may be having.

The bullying behaviour is a reflection of what is going on inside Brown's mind. When Brown fails to perform to the standards of his idealised view of himself, his ego is attacked and punished by a very severe superego. In his mind, Brown's failure to conform to his ideal effectively means that he will not be loved.

The roots of this conflict may be found in Brown's childhood in Kirkcaldy, Scotland. He had an especially strong tie with his parents, calling them his "inspiration". His father was a minister of the Church of Scotland and had a powerful influence on Brown, instilling within him a strong sense of fairness and social justice.

Brown accompanied his father on his rounds of parishioners and was exposed to the poverty and unemployment that resulted from the collapse of the textile and mining industries. These experiences led to Brown's interest in socialism and a firm political view that individuals are by nature primarily co-operative rather than self-centred.

Brown's ideal of serving the interests of the community over self-interests has informed much of his fiscal and social politics. However, it may well have become a tyrannical ideal within Brown's mind that has prevented him from being able to tolerate his own needs and weaknesses in the face of conflict. The shadow to Brown's idealism is a stern Calvinism that castigates selfishness and weakness.

When accused of hitting an aide, it is telling that Brown defended himself by referring to his father. Brown says, "I never heard him say an unkind word about anyone." From this, we can see that Brown's father represented an ideal for him that he has staunchly tried to follow. To be loved by his adored father means to be as close to this ideal as possible.

But it is an ideal that does not allow for anger or aggression. In short, it does not allow him to be human. And this is the problem.

The accusations against Brown concern his disregard for junior staff and people working for him in lowly positions, his indecisiveness, his difficulty in considering alternative views once he has made a decision, his difficulty in listening to criticism, his difficulty in commanding loyalty from his own Cabinet ministers and backbench MPs, and his difficulty in forming a strong vision of the country's future.

Each of these shortcomings is a result of Brown's persecutory inner world in which the demands he makes on himself have become crippling and abusive. Within such an internal straitjacket, it is hardly surprising that Brown is afraid of making decisions, afraid of hearing criticisms, and lacks the imaginative capacity to form an inspiring vision of the future.

Christine Pratt, head of the National Bullying Helpline, who claimed on Sunday that her charity had received phone calls from staff inside Number Ten, was concerned that Downing Street was so quick to deny any suggestion of bullying. She argued: "We would have hoped that Gordon Brown said he was looking into this, that due process was being followed and that he takes these issues seriously ... We would want Gordon Brown to follow the statutory code, the ACAS code, that he himself introduced."

Rather than relieving public concern, the denial issued by Number Ten on behalf of Brown only suggests fear: a fear of failing that cannot be admitted because it would mean, in Brown's mind, losing his father's love. The final irony is that in denying his behaviour, Brown is actually risking losing the following of his own constituency.

23 February 2010

44

Less clever men are more likely to cheat. Really?

Ashley Cole, John Terry, and Tiger Woods, now famous for their infidelities, are not very clever. It's not just that they got caught—which is never clever—and attracted a bad press. They have shown how unintelligent they are simply by being unfaithful.

That's if you believe the London Sschool of Economics evolutionary psychologist Satoshi Kanazawa who argues that men with lower IQs are more likely to be unfaithful than smarter guys.

Dr Kanazawa, whose report was published this week in the *Social Psychology Quarterly*, also claims that men with higher IQs are more likely to be atheist and politically liberal. In short, his message is that people with higher IQs are more "evolved" in their behaviour.

The research findings are drawn from a longitudinal study conducted in the US using a large sample of adolescents who were interviewed in 1994–1995 and again in 2001–2002 when they were between eighteen and twenty-eight years old. Data was also drawn from a cross-national study in the US. The young adults who saw themselves as "very liberal" scored an average IQ of 106, and those who saw themselves as "very conservative" had an average IQ of 95. The adolescents who were atheists had an average IQ of 103, whereas adults who were religious scored an average IQ of 97.

The significance of the difference in IQ scores is arguable and considered by many researchers to be only slight. IQ tests are also highly contentious sources of data for social studies and have been under attack for years. They are used most reliably in testing for educational difficulties amongst school-age children but, even with more sophisticated IQ tests, they cannot factor in all the variables that affect intelligence or necessarily agree on what intelligence is.

Kanazawa is well known for the startling conclusions he has made by extrapolating data from IQ surveys. In an article published in 2006, he claimed that attractive people are twenty-six per cent less likely to have male offspring. Three years earlier, he produced findings that showed scientists make their most important discoveries in their mid-thirties and, similarly, criminals are most productive at this age.

Kanazawa assumes that greater intelligence is linked with increased chances of success and survival. However, Kanazawa created most controversy when he coined the term "Savanna principle", referring to his theory that the societal difficulties we face now can be attributed to the fact that the human brain was evolved in Africa thousands of years ago in an environment entirely different from that in which we live today.

Critics of Kanazawa—of which there are many in academic circles—accuse him of questionable data, flawed assumptions, and inappropriate analyses resulting in biased and inadequate interpretations. The most serious criticism is that Kanazawa uses statistical associations as evidence of causality, as in the astounding links he makes in his new study.

Perhaps the most striking assumption that Kanazawa makes as an evolutionary psychologist is that there are signs that our morals and religious and political beliefs are evolving in adaptation to our changing environment.

On the subject of sexual exclusivity, for example, Kanazawa argues that men have always been "mildly polygamous" throughout evolutionary history because it was important to widen the genetic pool. Women, on the other hand, whose IQ scores had no bearing on their sexual fidelity, have always tended towards sexual exclusivity because of child-bearing and their need for male protection.

Now that these evolutionary pressures have diminished, Kanazawa concludes that intelligent people are more likely to adopt new practices that are beneficial in evolutionary terms.

Just as sexual exclusivity is a more evolved response to our environment today than infidelity, Kanazawa extends this argument to religion and politics. With regard to religion, Kanazawa argues that this, too, is a leftover from our evolutionary past as it is principally based on paranoia.

Humans needed to be paranoid in order to protect themselves from the dangers in their environment. Paranoia gives rise to a belief in an omnipotent protector. Conservatives are also environmental relics because their values are self-interested and therefore "primitive" in Kanazawa's eyes. And so the story goes.

There are several disturbing assumptions that underlie Kanazawa's version of evolutionary psychology. He assumes there is such a thing as moral development that can be identified over time as an environmental adaptation, that greater intelligence (as measured by IQ tests) is linked with increased chances of success and survival, and that sexual exclusivity, atheism, and liberalism are all superior in evolutionary terms as compared with their inferior counterparts.

Kanazawa does have his supporters. James Bailey, a leadership professor from George Washington University, agrees that "the adoption of some evolutionary novel ideas makes some sense in terms of moving the species forward. It also makes perfect sense that more intelligent people—people with, sort of, more intellectual power—are likely to be the ones to do that."

However, if Kanazawa and his supporters are right, we might expect to be living in an increasingly enlightened and cooperative world. Unfortunately, there seem to be few signs that we are evolving in this way. In fact, the evidence is dire. War and violence are ever-present dangers in our lives, and there is little evidence of lessening of evil in the world.

We only have to look around at our politicians, who presumably have a reasonably high IQ (or at least we might hope so), to see how many are conservative, religious, and unfaithful to their wives. There is also no indication that humans are any less unfaithful than we were a hundred or two hundred or three hundred years ago. It is likely that the reverse is true, especially given the modern advances in birth-control methods.

Kanazawa's view of human behaviour lacks any recognition that there are not only situational pressures but unconscious factors that create behaviour patterns.

An example of this was when the Berlin Wall came down and there was an expectation that the East Berliners would respond to their liberation positively. The opposite happened as depression set in. There was a marked rise in the number of suicides committed by young men as well as a marked increase in abortions among young women. What had not been factored in was the psychological effect of emerging from a tyrannical and paranoid regime and having to face the destructiveness, hatred, and loss that had been suffered and the hopelessness this created.

Kanazawa is reducing the complexity of our psychological lives in order to try to prove his theory that human psychology is developing. He is also promoting the view that evolution entails the development from something "primitive" into something "superior".

Both of these assumptions are not only unproven but dangerous. In effect, Kanazawa is putting a moral spin on evolutionary development that is reminiscent of Hitler's arguments for social eugenics. So is sexual infidelity passé, or is it evolutionary psychology that we need to evolve out of?

3 March 2010

45

Why Jon Venables wants to reveal his true identity

Jon Venables' compulsion to disclose his identity is rooted in his sense of guilt and need for punishment

Jon Venables and Robert Thompson were found guilty of killing the toddler Jamie Bulger in 1993. The youngest people to be jailed for murder in English history, they were released from custody under licence in 2001. Both were given government protection of new identities so they could live a normal life outside prison with guaranteed anonymity. This protection was first granted to Mary Bell in similar circumstances.

Now aged twenty-seven, Venables has been recalled to prison for breaching his licence. The Justice Secretary will not reveal the nature of his violation, but press rumours suggest variously that he beat someone up at work, that he was seen in Liverpool clubs chatting up girls when he is banned from Merseyside, and/or that he has been caught snorting coke.

The most serious allegation, reported on Sunday, is that he committed an offence involving child pornography. There is no confirmation of any of these violations, but it is clear that the breach must have been serious for Venables to be recalled to prison.

What is undoubtedly of great concern, and curiosity, is that Venables has been telling people who he really is. He has been described as being in a state of "persistent self-disclosure", in which he has felt increasingly compelled to disclose his real identity to others, including strangers.

Having disclosed his identity to fellow prisoners and prison staff, he is now being held in isolation due to his deteriorating mental condition. There is also the fear that his real identity will become widely known throughout the prison system—putting him at great risk.

A new identity costs the government approximately £250,000 to create. There is also an emotional cost to the person who takes up a new identity. "Double lives are a burden for people", Ian Cumming, a consultant forensic psychiatrist, explains. The secrecy itself "takes its toll", but there is the further burden of what Dr Cumming describes as "the national demonisation of an individual".

While leading a double life is something that most of us would abhor, except in our occasional fantasy, in the case of Venables it is vital for self-preservation. So why tell?

There is a somewhat confused picture of Venables' mental state at the time of his conviction. During their incarceration, before trial, it was Thompson who was described as the psychopath. Venables, on the other hand, cried frequently and suffered from nightmares in which he saw James Bulger in his room. He was also held up by staff as being a role model for other young offenders.

However, during their trial, it was revealed that it was Venables who first suggested to Thompson, "Let's get a kid lost", and who told the adults who stopped him as he was leading the distressed Bulger by the hand through the shopping mall that he was his "little brother". Hours later, Bulger had been beaten to death by the two ten-year-olds on a railway line. Although by this account, Venables was in charge, he was also the one who suffered the most subsequently.

As a child, Venables had a history of trouble-making and disturbed behaviour at school. He once attacked another child so ferociously that it took two teachers to separate them. His mother was violent and suffered from depression, his two siblings had special needs, and there was no father in the household. It is arguable that his eight years in custody would in many respects have equipped him to deal with the difficulties of life better than his family could have done.

Since his release from prison, claims have been made that Venables has become a heavy drinker, uses drugs, and has been involved in confrontations and fights. Venables would most certainly have received some form of rehabilitative care in custody, but the nature of this care is not reported. Whatever therapy was provided, it does not seem to have been effective in keeping Venables' demons at bay.

It is most likely that Venables' compulsion to disclose his identity is rooted in his sense of guilt and need for punishment. His murderous attack on a younger child indicates an intense hatred and envy of a child whom he may have perceived as loved and wanted in comparison to his own experience of life.

His own unconscious guilt was manifest in his nightmares immediately following Bulger's murder. The spectre of what he has done and his self-loathing are clearly just as alive and virulent today as they were when he was a boy of ten—perhaps even more so.

For someone who is not psychopathic and who feels remorse and concern, having to continue to hide their crime may well drive them insane. It is ironic that, by all reports, Thompson, who was described as psychopathic, seems in contrast to have settled into his new life.

Venables' apparent self-destructiveness may be his attempt to seek some form of acceptance of who he really is and a release from his internal persecution. There is the conflicting hope of being forgiven along with a darker desire for the murderer within him to be destroyed. He seems to be looking for a parent who will excise his sins and restore him to the world and the possibility of being loved, even if it is at the cost of his own life.

The predicament for Venables is that he has destroyed his chance of living a normal life under his own identity. This is not only a loss that is inconceivable for most of us, but it is a loss that he must find some way of coming to terms with in order to truly create a new identity and a new life.

8 March 2010

46
Chatroulette and perverts who want to attack mother

**The random video chat website is a hothouse of
what Freud called "paraphilia"**

Click on to chatroulette.com, activate your webcam, and it is pure chance as to whether you will see a demure girl wanting to chat, a couple having sex, an overweight middle-aged man asking what the weather is like in London, a young man masturbating to the camera, or a party where you're invited to dance along with the music.

Chatroulette is the new live chat website, launched last November, and the ultimate in social networking. It is free, unregulated, and, most important, the video chats are with random strangers. All the viewer has to do is to click "next" and another person will come onto the screen and another adventure unfold.

Initially the founder of Chatroulette was unknown. But last month, *Andrey Ternovskiy*, a seventeen-year-old student from Moscow, came out as its creator. Bored with the predictability of internet chat lines, Ternovskiy invented a social site along the lines of Russian roulette that ensures constant novelty and opens up the possibility of an unlimited fantasy life with which no other website can compete.

Worldwide user numbers have soared from more than 35,000 concurrent users last month to a recent count of over

1.5 million and growing. It is particularly popular amongst the student population in the US, but it is spreading rapidly in European and Asian countries as well.

Ternovskiy wanted to create a site that could fulfil the different needs and desires of a variety of users. "Some think it is a game", he says, "others think it is a whole unknown world, others think it is a dating service". The point of it is to draw people together from around the world.

But because of its anonymity, it has inevitably attracted scores of users who are more interested in its potential for sex games than for social networking.

The New York film-maker Casey Neistat conducted a brief survey of Chatroulette and found that of the ninety people he clicked through on a Thursday afternoon in New York, seventy-one per cent were men, fifteen per cent were women, fourteen per cent perverts (undefined), eighty-three per cent were fairly young, and seventeen per cent were older users. He also found that he was "nexted" by ninety-five per cent of his viewers, while a female friend had a far lower rate of five per cent who clicked her away.

The combination of randomness and anonymity has produced an exciting recipe that is described as "surreal", "frightening", "creepy", "overwhelming", and, ultimately, "addictive". At the click of a computer key, the user can have a glimpse of the intimate aspects of someone else's life and can reveal the most personal and secret aspects of theirs.

Users can be voyeurs (just point your webcam at the cat or the wall) or exhibitionists or both. The site breaks down the barriers between public and private, and conveys a sense of an "uncontrollable frontier" in which you can do anything and say anything with anyone. The only barrier is the computer screen itself.

Freud coined the term "paraphilia" to describe perverse sexual behaviour that is literally outside or beyond the bounds of love.

There are two basic forms of paraphilia. One is described as "hands off", meaning that there is no actual touch involved and gratification is achieved primarily visually. The other form of "paraphilia" involves partners that are either inappropriate (such as children or animals) or non-consenting. Whatever form it may take, the distinctive feature of paraphilia is that the object of desire is de-personalised and is used like an actor in a film to play a certain role that is both exciting and gratifying to the subject/director.

One example of this is the male exhibitionist who, in displaying his penis to unsuspecting women, acts out a specific fantasy. He is asserting his masculinity in the eyes of a mother by whom he has felt castrated. By projecting his mother randomly onto other women, his act serves a whole set of psychological impulses. It is an attack against the mother, a reaffirmation of the man's masculine identity, and there is an omnipotent excitement about defying the law—in metaphorical terms, the father.

This is the kind of unconscious scenario that we may unwittingly stumble upon at the next click of Chatroulette.

The addictive quality of this kind of behaviour lies in the fact that the object of desire is reduced from a real person into an object. As such, the object can never be destroyed, and it is stripped of the capacity to feel anything but excitement. There is no person to feel concerned about, and this also means there is no person to love or to be loved by.

There is little lasting satisfaction because the partner is only a fantasy, and it is this that creates an addictive longing for more. It is precisely Chatroulette's anonymity, and the de-personalisation that accompanies this, that makes it so addictive, and successful.

Chatroulette is an ideal visual playground for the "hands off" exhibitionist and voyeur. Both can trawl through the site in search of their perfect fantasy match, and the players can be replenished and replaced at any time.

Chatroulette is not only appealing to the exhibitionists and voyeurs who are looking for their fantasy partners and who presumably constitute fourteen per cent of its users. It is also a place where others, not looking for a sexual high, can "surf" through people and situations much in the same way as shoppers surf the net for bargains.

The imaginal universe has no boundaries and it is far better than the virtual-reality sites, such as Second Life, because it is real life—or close to it. But it is real life on a two-dimensional plane. Contacts are fleeting and elusive and can be deleted instantly. It is like telling one's life story to a fellow passenger on a train, knowing that he is getting off at the next stop.

Under the protection of anonymity, we can experiment with our identities, explore our fantasies, and enter worlds different from our own. This can most certainly enrich our psychological growth and our understanding of others. But we may also be reassured that the allure of anonymity has a transient appeal.

Even Ternovskiy, who was originally as anonymous as the users of his site, could not resist for long revealing his real identity and taking credit for his creation.

25 March 2010

47

The spread of rape spells madness in the Congo

Soldiers in DR Congo are notorious rapists. Why has this behaviour spread to civilian men?

The Democratic Republic of Congo is notorious for brutality and violence—and especially rape and other sexual assaults committed by soldiers. Alarmingly, the rapists are no longer confined to the military. A study released by Oxfam says that in 2008, thirty-eight per cent of the rapes reported across the country were committed by civilians, as compared with fewer than one per cent in 2004.

To explain the spread of sexual violence in the civilian population, it is important to question first of all why it is so prevalent among soldiers. For this is where the sexual violence has so far gone unchecked.

Within the Congo, there is no government legal structure that is either effective or that has the recognised support of the various constituencies. Without a protective authority—or, in psychological terms, a potent father—there are few restraints to curb violence and aggression.

The situation is similar to an individual lacking a healthy super-ego that prevents him from falling prey to destructive impulses.

The result in the Congo seems to be the proliferation of gang affiliations that maintain their own authority through fear and intimidation.

Many of the country's soldiers have had to witness extreme violence. They have also been forced by superiors to commit acts of violence *and* been subjected to violence themselves. To survive all this psychologically, they have identified with the aggressor and adopted the norms of the gang culture.

When feelings of hatred, fear, and aggression become mentally overwhelming, one way of trying to get rid of them is by eroticising them. The soldier who rapes is actively triumphing over the weak, frightened, and defenceless part of himself, as projected onto his victim. The sadism involved in this act becomes exciting and addictive in itself, and is adhered to increasingly as the ego becomes more and more frightened and endangered.

This has nothing to do with sexuality; it has to do with a way of expelling violent feelings that cannot be contained within the self into another.

It is also possible to see sexual violence as the soldiers' reaction to feeling castrated and powerless. The fact that rape has become so widespread suggests that it is rapidly becoming part of a process of mass institutionalisation and normalisation within the different factions fighting one another.

The civilian population is even more impotent than the soldiers who are fighting when it comes to protecting themselves. Just as there has been an increase in the incidence and severity of sexual violence committed by soldiers, it should be no surprise that there has been a steep rise in civilian rape.

When husbands and fathers witness the rape of their wives and daughters and, increasingly, have been raped themselves, they too are at risk of being infected by the hatred that has been passed on to them. In their impotence, civilian men may be attempting to reclaim some sense of power, however illusory, by inflicting pain and punishing those who are weaker than themselves. Vulnerability is attacked as a way to destroy feeling.

Violence is traumatic in any form and its victims often perpetuate and incite further violence, inflicting what has been done to them onto others. This is the case regardless of whether it is institutionalised violence or domestic violence.

When there is a culture of such violence, it inevitably pervades the cultural psyche and permeates into domestic relations where it can be even more destructive in its long-term damage to family structure and future generations. What we are seeing in the Congo is just this—that at the most fundamental level, love between men and women is being perverted into hate. When this begins to happen, the culture is truly in danger of becoming mad.

16 April 2010

48

None of the party leaders is offering us charisma

Clegg comes closest, but we're too self-interested to accept his vision

When Gordon Brown took over from Tony Blair as prime minister and leader of the Labour Party in 2007, there were many who welcomed the prospect of a "real" figure becoming PM, in contrast to what they saw as the artifice and charisma of the Blair years.

Brown did not put on a media face or appear to make false promises. It was Brown's "realness", along with his Calvinist principles, that was meant to restore faith in the Labour Party and accountability within government.

But a series of blunders—culminating in "Bigot-gate"—and rumours about his character traits have tarnished Brown. He has become only too "real", it seems, and while some may still regard him with sympathy, many are asking—as the opinion polls make clear—whether this is the kind of behaviour we want in a prime minister.

In other words, was the sort of charisma offered by Tony Blair such a bad thing, after all?

In 1956, an American television show called *To Tell the Truth* made its debut, and it remained one of the most popular shows for more than a decade. Three panellists played the part of someone who had an extraordinary job or an unusual experience.

Two panellists were imposters and the third was the real person. Four celebrities were given the job of trying to catch out who were the imposters through a series of questions. The imposters were allowed to lie, but the real person was sworn to tell the truth. At the end of the show, the real contestant was asked to stand up. Surprisingly, the contestant the celebrities voted for was more often than not one of the imposters. The clear message was that the power of illusion is stronger than reality.

The first of the recent televised leaders' debates set the tone for what was to bear a remarkable resemblance to *To Tell the Truth*. Being "real" no longer matters: what matters is how convincing the contestants are. What also matters is who performs best, who has the best rhetoric, and ultimately, who presents the most optimistic view of the future.

Now that we have weathered the shock of the market collapse, Britain is only just beginning to feel its impact. This is a time when, logically, we need a strong father figure to secure greater monetary controls and to protect the poor and the unemployed while working out a realistic national budget for the future.

But a strong father would also point out that things are much more likely to get worse than better and that our economic and social reality may be changing in fundamental ways that it is hard for us to imagine. The strong father, like a competent manager, would do his best to get his family to face reality and its limitations.

This is never popular election talk. The French psychoanalyst Didier Anzieu claims that any group situation inevitably gives rise to hallucinatory wish-fulfilment. Groups tend to regress psychologically and trigger off our earliest narcissistic desires. The group itself can also come to represent a place in which all wishes will be satisfied. The group looks for a leader who will not only stand for the "ego ideal"—the ideal that most of us strive to be like—but who will promote the illusion that all will be well and that the paradise we have known in our past will be restored in a new form.

Typically, groups will favour illusion over reality. This also means that they will favour the visionary leader over the father figure. In fact, part of the appeal of the aspiring leader is that, like the hero he is meant to be, he has come to vanquish the old order, to vanquish the father, and to take his place.

So how do the contestants in this general election line up in the illusions they are offering?

Brown is certainly presenting a rosier future that will require only a temporary cinching in of our belts before prosperity returns. As the former chancellor, he is trying to convince us that he has the best formula for recovery.

However, no degree of illusion can at this stage ameliorate his reputation—whether deserved or not—as a bully who has little empathy with others. Although his illusions may be appealing, his "real" personality, along with the negatives of the last thirteen years under Labour—the Iraq war, the expenses scandal, and so on—undermine his appeal. He simply can't carry off the illusion.

David Cameron, on the other hand, is depicting a future largely in terms of restoring the past, focusing on its privileges and not its hardships. What has been lost under Labour can be regained, he says. Everything can be like it was—if not better.

But Cameron's illusion is flawed primarily because it harks back to the past and because he acknowledges the difficulties that lie ahead in achieving this. In short, his illusion is not visionary, it is retrospective, if not reactionary. The reason why Cameron is not seriously winning over the electorate—he is ahead in the polls, but only just—may well reflect this weakness. It is not an illusion that presents itself as a new solution.

Nick Clegg's rise to stardom as a result of the first leaders' debate most likely indicates the population's search for a charismatic leader who will offer them a convincing illusion that they can hold on to. However, the spotlight on Clegg has been relatively short-lived, and this may also reflect the *kind* of vision he is promoting.

Clegg is advocating a much more inclusive worldview than either of the other candidates. His emphasis on "fairness", as evident in his proposal to give amnesty to immigrants already living in this country, extends the limits of the group beyond our own immediate self-interests. While, as Clegg argues, we may have to "get real" and accept this, it does not speak to the narcissistic desires of the group who want, if anything, to be assured of their dominance.

From the polls, it is becoming increasingly evident that voters are no longer interested in politicians being "real" people. Nor is there much appeal in presenting a "real" prognosis of the future. Artifice and illusion seem to be what we want from our leaders, especially in these difficult times.

None of the candidates is able to produce an illusion that is powerful enough to be convincing, which is why, with only days to go, this election remains such a close race.

As Bud Collyer, the host of *To Tell the Truth*, would say, "And now will the real prime minister please stand up?"

4 May 2010

49

TV's virgin auctions: who pays the highest price?

The new reality show hosted by a Nevada brothel

It will be reassuring to some to know that virginity is still highly prized in our society. But now there's a new twist. Plans for a reality television programme in which young people auction off their virginity to the highest bidder are underway in Nevada.

Justin Sisley, an Australian documentary-maker, moved the programme to the desert state after he was told that Australian authorities would prosecute him for prostitution if filming went ahead in the state of Victoria. The show is being hosted by a Nevada brothel.

Sisley claims to have found at least three willing virgins for his programme. Each is being offered $20,000 along with ninety per cent of the "sale price", the remainder going to the brothel. Initially, bids will be placed online, and only the final round of bidders will appear on television where they will appear face to face with the virgin they are hoping to buy.

Both men and women virgins are volunteering and profess different motives, although the large pay-off is a significant factor.

"Veronica", aged twenty-one, wants to earn money while at the same time promoting feminist views about women's sexuality—although it is not entirely clear what these views might be.

Evelyn Duenas, aged twenty-eight, a cleaner from Ecuador, wants to raise money for the care of her mother, who is suffering from Alzheimer's, and to fund her own studies. The government in Ecuador is so concerned about the situation that they are seriously considering contributing to her mother's care and to her studies in order to prevent Evelyn's participation in the show.

The third of the trio of virgins is a young man called "Alex", who says he simply wants to meet someone.

As for the bidders, we have no idea who they will be or how they will describe their motives.

The announcement of the programme has been received with outrage and curiosity. The fact that it is being hosted by a brothel only underscores the fact that the transaction is a form of prostitution—and traditionally, virgins fetch the highest prices in this profession.

The two female volunteers make it clear that they are doing it for financial reasons—a means to an end. Unfortunately, most prostitutes start out thinking the same thing. But the experience is so debasing that they often get hooked as a way of denying what they are doing to themselves and how they are being treated. Once people dissociate from their feelings, it is a very hard process to reverse.

Virginity is the ultimate commodity because it represents purity and innocence. The reward in Islam for being a devout Muslim is to go to heaven and to be surrounded by seventy-two virgins, representing different aspects of paradise and God's ecstasy. In most religions, virginity exemplifies purity of spirit and all that is untouched by badness. Virginity confers satisfaction of a spiritual order rather than a sexual one and symbolises pure love.

Historically, most cultures have held to the tradition that a wife needed to be a virgin on her wedding night. This has not only ensured that the patriliny has been kept intact along with the wealth of the family, but it has also been a form of social contract to protect women. In exchange for his wife's virginity—and fecundity—the husband is bound to care and provide for her and her children.

While women's position in most Western societies has changed radically, it is perhaps the advent of modern forms of birth control that has most challenged the importance we place on virginity. Sex and its consequences can be separated much more readily than ever before.

However, one's first sexual experience marks an important step in psychological development. It is an initiation into adulthood with the attendant responsibilities of parenting. To minimise the importance of one's first sexual partner is a way of attacking the mutual dependency that is an inevitable ingredient of any sexual relationship, no matter how much this may be denied or wished away.

What is so disturbing about Sisley's programme is that it invites the public to participate in the perversion of virginity. As a powerful symbol of love, virginity is debased and turned into a mere object that can be auctioned like a new car.

Sisley's programme undoubtedly appeals to the omnipotent delinquent viewer in us all. The other person doesn't matter, there is no responsibility, there is just pleasure and greed and an illusion of power. Above all, feelings of vulnerability and emotional need are denigrated. As long as the ends are stated to be for a good cause, then who cares how they're achieved? Volunteers and bidders alike can fool themselves with the idea that everyone comes out a winner.

Like a naughty kid, Sisley admits that the parents of the people involved "hate me". Do we detect a note of triumph here?

12 May 2010

50

Derrick Bird: mentality of a suicide bomber

What makes a suicide killer take others with him?

The night before taxi driver Derrick Bird went on his killing spree in west Cumbria, he had an argument at his taxi rank and drove away saying: "You won't see me again." This was the first clue that Bird had planned his suicide—and the shootings the next day.

Bird's victims were not all random. The first victims—his twin brother and the family solicitor who is thought to have been involved in drawing up his mother's will—were both shot in their homes. Three other victims were fellow taxi drivers. Bird had been under particular stress recently as his ninety-year-old mother, who is seriously ill, had been staying with him between periods in a nursing home. It is now thought that a row over his mother's will triggered the shootings.

Bird's elaborate drive along the Cumbrian coast from Whitehaven, shooting at different locations until he stopped in Boot, where he abandoned his car and shot himself, suggests that it is highly likely that he had in some way also mapped out his route and may well have had fantasies of the shooting spree—and of his particular victims—long before enacting it.

It is very likely that Bird's victims were, at least in terms of his unconscious, not random at all. We can see some of the seeds of Bird's shooting spree in his past. He was a loner, a trait that is often associated with men who commit spree killings. He also knew how to handle guns. He had grown up hunting with his father and inherited his shotguns.

Most important, his murder of his twin brother, followed by the murder of the family solicitor, suggests that there was intense rivalry between the siblings that could well have reached a climax with their mother's impending death.

Bird's separation from his wife has been attributed to his wish for her to have an abortion with her second pregnancy which she refused to do. This may be some indication that he could only tolerate one child and that another child presented too much of a rivalrous threat to him.

But what about all the other people Bird shot? Were they merely victims of Bird's uncontrollable rage and omnipotent destructiveness?

Although we can only speculate on Bird's motivations for the shootings, what is common in such acts of violence is that there is a detailed fantasised scenario that is being enacted. Each character in the scenario counts.

Just as Bird charted the locations of his final drive, it is also very likely that his victims were, at least in terms of his unconscious, not random at all but represented internal characters with whom he was in conflict.

The young man cutting a hedge, the older woman crossing the road, the driver who stopped beside him, may well have set off associations with people in his life that appeared in his mind. Each time someone is killed, there is yet someone else who threatens. As Freud wrote, "There is no death in the unconscious." This gives us some way of understanding why Bird went on a killing spree and why he knew he had to kill himself in the end.

The fantasised scenario is also played out before an audience. The message may be as simple as, "See what I can do, who I can destroy, how powerful I am", or it may be more complicated, depending on the internal relationships at work. Lying behind the scenario is an overwhelming experience of impotence that fosters murderous feelings. The result is an emotional time bomb that is waiting to be set off.

The final suicidal act is a natural ending. While some theories suggest that suicide in these cases is committed out of guilt, it is more likely that it is actually the ultimate psychic murder of a hated internal object that is sought. In effect, the actual killings do not quench the murderous feelings but exacerbate them. While the murders are committed out of impotent rage, there is also an unconscious masochistic desire to be one with a loving internal figure who requires total submission.

The psychological parallel with suicide bombers is striking. The aim of the terrorist is to be loved, either by God or by the leader of the terrorist cell, or both, by submitting himself completely to his power.

The murderous feelings towards the parent—in the case of the terrorist, it is normally the father—are then split off and directed towards the "other" and ultimately towards the self in the suicidal act. The terrorist is also killing off what is "other", "alien", and impure within himself. Internal conflict is eradicated by an attempt to wipe out everyone who represents a threat to narcissistic supremacy.

Bird's terrorist was undoubtedly inside his mind and became so powerful that he could no longer resist his commands. His murderous acts may have held out the promise that he would in the end fulfil his omnipotent desire of being the only one.

Had Bird wanted to be his mother's only beloved? It is Bird's mother who has lived to witness his carnage. Was she his audience of one?

4 June 2010

51

Congress *vs.* Hayward: how it became a witch hunt

The xenophobic fantasy behind the oil spill outrage

The heckling began as soon as BP's chief executive, Tony Hayward, opened his mouth to address the US Congress at yesterday's hearing. A shrimper from Texas, her hands covered in oil, immediately accused Hayward of being a criminal and had to be forcibly removed from the chamber.

But the heckling also came from congressmen. Democrat Henry Waxman portrayed Hayward as "cavalier", while Republican Michael Burgess expressed his fear that Hayward might be in charge of other oil wells around the world, suggesting that the BP chief executive was putting the world at risk.

Perhaps the most vociferous attack came from Bart Stupak, a Michigan Democrat, who accused Hayward of taking "a golden parachute back to England [while] we in America are left to recover for years from the disaster".

This nationalist remark reveals the paranoid fantasy that is emerging that it is foreigners who have caused this damage and who must be extradited in order to protect the safety of the nation.

Although BP has succumbed to the Obama administration's demand to set up an escrow account of up to $20 billion to fund compensation claims, this has not quenched the desire to single out a fall-guy. The congressional accusations have shown a determination to prove Hayward guilty before the trial has begun.

This indicates what in psychoanalytic terms would be called the paranoid-schizoid position, in which all badness is split off and projected onto someone else so that the self can remain all good. The reason why this is called "paranoia" is that it then leads to a fear that others are out to get you. In other words, there must be someone to blame for whatever disaster occurs.

The witch-hunt mentality that has taken over Washington's response to the oil spill—and much of the media reaction it—is particularly evident in the much-quoted comparison made by Obama between the oil spill disaster and the 9/11 terrorist attack. A cartoon of al-Qaeda admiring BP for masterminding such an effective attack against the US says it all.

However, this is a gross distortion of what Obama actually said. On 14 June, the president told the political website Politico: "In the same way that our view of our vulnerabilities and our foreign policy was shaped profoundly by 9/11, I think this disaster is going to shape how we think about the environment and energy for many years to come." Obama's message was quite clearly that the disaster is a wake-up call that has shaken the American belief in its own invincibility.

The president seems to have touched on a raw nerve in the American psyche that has its historical antecedents in its Puritan beginnings and, above all, in the extreme vulnerability of the early settlers who had to survive in the face of a wilderness that was life-threatening.

When a group is vulnerable and its existence is endangered, for whatever reason, it normally responds by demonising one of its members. He or she then becomes the symbolic scapegoat who must be sacrificed in order to purify the group and re-establish safety and an illusion of control.

The Salem witch trials of 1692–1693 are a prime example of this process. They were largely a response to a variety of conflicts—economic, religious, and political—that were besetting the New England colony.

The witch hunt arises as a way of splitting off the conflict by investing it with the form of an external enemy. The fight against the enemy then enables the different warring factions to band together and, at least for a time, to form some sort of unity.

The BP disaster may be politically timely in so far as it has happened in the midst of what seem to be growing schisms within the US, both political and economic.

More importantly, in a shaky economy that is no way near out of recession, a disastrous mistake such as the Deepwater spill is a ready target for anger and blame. Like al-Qaeda, the root of the disaster lies outside the US and not within the country.

But while the accusations fly against Tony Hayward, there has been one notable dissenter.

Republican congressman Joe Barton apologised yesterday to BP for the £20 billion escrow account it has been asked to create. Emphasising that he was only speaking for himself, Barton said, "I think it is a tragedy of the first proportion that a private corporation can be subjected to what I would characterise as a shakedown."

To the horror of his fellow committee members there to give Hayward a roasting, Barton went on to describe the escrow account as "a $20bn slush fund that's unprecedented in our nation's history, that's got no legal standing, and which sets, I think, a terrible precedent for the future".

Barton was clearly criticising the Obama administration—*he was later forced by his party whip to apologise*—but he was also pointing out the dangers inherent in a "shakedown" that can easily serve to mask deeper problems that are not one person's or one company's responsibility alone.

In psychological development, the paranoid-schizoid position is followed by what is called the depressive position. This means that the self is able to own up to its own destructiveness and to feel guilt and concern for others and the impact of one's actions on others.

Our need to find a fall-guy on whom to pin the damage is not only an attempt to establish our innocence—it is also a way of avoiding our depression for the destructiveness that has been done, regardless of whose "fault" it is. Photographs of oil-soaked pelicans are a reminder of our collective destructiveness and not just the damage done by BP.

18 June 2010

52

Aimee Sword: the hate that turned to incestuous love

What made a thirty-six-year-old mother want to start an incestuous affair with her fourteen-year-old son?

Aimee Sword, an attractive thirty-six-year-old married woman, mother of five, was found guilty yesterday in a Detroit courtroom of incest with her fourteen-year-old son and sentenced to between nine and thirty years' imprisonment. Pleading guilty so that her son would not have to testify against her, Sword apologised to her children and her sister, saying, "I am remorseful for everything that occurred … I don't understand it."

Fourteen years after giving up her son for adoption, Aimee Sword contacted him through Facebook when the adoptive family failed to send her regular reports. Sword then asked the adoptive family if he could spend time with her in a hotel and visit her in her family home, to which they agreed.

This was the beginning of what became a tragic *folie à deux* between them. As her lawyer explained, "When she saw this boy—something touched off in her—it wasn't a mother–son relationship, it was a boyfriend–girlfriend relationship." He added, "Aimee's searching for a reason why this happened. She can't understand it. She's going to get some counselling."

It is hard for most of us to believe that a woman in her mid-thirties could see an adolescent boy as a boyfriend, and even harder if the boy happens to be her son. Yet the fact that she and her son convinced themselves that this was the case indicates a psychotic collusion between them that enabled them to commit incest on at least one occasion if not more.

Apart from murder, incest is the most taboo crime in our society—and incest between mother and son, its most prohibited form. Reporting and convictions of mother–son incest are relatively rare, and even self-report surveys show that the incidence is low by comparison with father–daughter and father–son incest.

While father–daughter incest most often comes to light as a result of the daughter's pregnancy, there is usually no such evidence to alert others in the case of mother–son incest. In Sword's case, it was her son who told his counsellor about their relationship.

As in the myth of Oedipus, what is horrifying about incest is that it signifies the killing of the father when the son usurps his role in his mother's bed. The natural order is destroyed—the difference between generations is wiped out, along with the need for protection and nurturance. Boundaries and limits are eradicated, and there is no authority to curb destructiveness.

The incestuous couple typically believe that they have a special, secret relationship which transcends the rules that govern other people's lives. It is a heady cocktail of the secret love affair that, being outside the law, offers an illusion of living with the gods. It is psychotic in the sense that external reality is denied. What is also denied is any feeling of hate.

Sword's lawyer emphasised that she did not see her son as her son. He said that "something touched off in her". This was the son whom she had rejected and never knew. She could use him to satisfy her own narcissistic needs without having to recognise her responsibility towards him as a parent. At the same time, she could mask her hatred for his vulnerability by eroticising the relationship. It is also highly likely that Sword was compelled unconsciously to repeat an incestuous relationship from her own past and to inflict the abuse she had suffered on her son, confusing love with hate.

Sword's son, adopted as an infant, could also mask his own inevitable feelings of hate towards his rejecting mother by becoming her "adult" sexual partner. Through their mad love affair, they could avoid having to know about or feel the pain and loss of what had actually happened to both of them.

It is an especially damaging experience for Sword's son. In most forms of parent–child incest, the child is passive. However, incest in adolescence requires the boy to be active, not passive, and entails the risk of impregnation. This risk is the most horrifying aspect of incest for boys psychologically.

The mother encourages the boy to take an active part not only in killing off/replacing the father but in giving her a child, replacing himself, and in this way abnegating his need for a mother. He is put into a position of denying his need for either parent. The boy then experiences an increase in castration anxiety and guilt that may become intolerable and in some instances can lead to suicide. When Oedipus found out that his wife was in fact his mother, he blinded himself with a pin from her dress.

While Aimee Sword will undoubtedly attempt to understand her own unconscious motivation in seducing her son, her son will be facing a different challenge. If he remains a victim, he will always be the abandoned child. If he can be helped to see his own hate and destructiveness, he will be able to accept the damage that has been done to him and his own guilt without the need to blind himself. There is no innocent victim in incest. As we can see in the story of Oedipus, the real danger is in blinding ourselves to our unconscious.

14 July 2010

53

Joanne Lee suicide pact: the comfort of strangers

Why two people who did not know each other might have joined up to kill themselves

The message posted on an internet suicide forum read: "I haven't the strength to do this alone. I'm not a cop, a cannibal, or a murderer, just desperate. I have all the ingredients and want to do it ASAP." It was written by thirty-four-year-old Joanne Lee who was found dead in a car this week on the industrial estate where she lived with her parents in Braintree, Essex.

With her was Steve Lumb, a lorry driver who had driven two hundred miles from his home in Sowerby, West Yorkshire, to join her in suicide. It is believed that they met for the first time only hours before they gassed themselves to death with a chemical cocktail that Lee had learned how to produce from the same internet site.

According to their families, there were few apparent signs that either Lee or Lumb were suicidal.

Lumb's father, with whom he lived, said of his son: "There was no depression and he never talked about taking his own life. He was a lovely lad." This was despite his mother's death two-and-a-half years ago. "I thought he had got over that," said his father, "everything seemed all right".

Similarly, Lee's parents described her as a "lovely daughter" and "very caring". They also claimed they had no idea that their daughter was having problems. Nevertheless, Joanne Lee had an eating disorder, and her neighbours described her as "painfully thin", to the point that she had begun to lose her teeth.

Both Lee's parents' and Lumb's father's reactions suggest that there was considerable denial within each family of anything that was going wrong with their children.

While it is possible only to speculate on the individual reasons behind these two suicides, the more puzzling question is why two strangers might arrange to meet with the sole purpose of killing themselves together. Two is company? Or is there more to it than that?

The Italian poet Cesare Pavese, who himself committed suicide, wrote, "Behind every suicide is a shy homicide." When murderous feelings towards others have to be suppressed, the only way to be rid of them is to turn them against the self.

It is especially taboo to feel murderous towards one[1]s parents, although they are also the most likely candidates as they have usually, and most often unwittingly, inflicted the greatest harm. Both Lee and Lumb were "lovely" children. There was no indication of anger or depression—except for Lee[1]s attempt to starve herself to death.

Although suicide is certainly a desperate act, it is also an act performed before an imaginary audience. The clichéd silent threat is, "You'll be sorry when I'm gone!" Harming oneself is a passive-aggressive attack against the person who has been hurtful.

What is different in the case of Lee is that she was looking for an accomplice to commit suicide with her. The fact that Lumb was so quick to the gun suggests that he, too, had been looking for an accomplice.

Lee asserts in her suicide note, "I am not a cop, a cannibal, or a murderer." She seems to be saying that she cannot control her hatred (she is not a cop), she is fearful of her cannibalistic feelings (she is starving herself to death), and she is also fearful of her murderous feelings (she is not a murderer).

Her need to find someone to give her the strength to kill herself may be a need for someone to validate her hatred and her desperation, to absolve her from feeling guilty, or to give her the illusion that she will not be abandoned at death—that in entering death with someone else, she will continue to be loved.

Whatever may have been Lee's fantasy, she surely had one that included someone else, as did Lumb.

We know that Lee had specifically set the date of 30 August to kill herself, explaining, "It's a special date for me. I was born on the 30th January. I came in on the 30th, so I will go out on the 30th. I've never been so excited." As it happened, she overshot her deadline by three weeks—because she could not enlist her accomplice soon enough.

But her excitement about "going out" on the same date that she "came in" suggests an attack against the mother who gave birth to her. The fact that she needed an accomplice—and the fact that she found a man to join her—further suggests that she may also have been excited about a fantasy that she and her father could kill off her mother and live happily ever after in death. The perfect Oedipal triumph.

For his part, Lumb may have had a similar fantasy as he jumped at the chance to come to the aid of Lee. In killing himself, he may have wanted to join his late mother. His Oedipal triumph.

We cannot know what fantasy exactly brought these two people together. But we do know that, on a psychological level, there was some internal drama that was being enacted that required the participation of someone else.

The fact that Lee and Lumb were strangers may have been an advantage. Being strangers, they could both be stand-ins, acting out their own respective dramas that happened to coincide.

It is as if Lee, in searching the internet site, had sent out a call to central casting to supply the missing actor she needed to make her play go ahead. And Lumb fitted the part.

The real mystery in the story is how successful the unconscious can be in finding its perfect match.

22 September 2010

54

The guilt that binds Ed and David Miliband together

Just as in the story of Jacob and Esau, the older brother has been robbed of his birthright

Ed Miliband's victory over his older brother David to win the Labour Party leadership plays out the archetypal drama of sibling rivalry that ends with the defeat of the older generation. This is the basic taboo that Ed Miliband has broken, the wish that has been fulfilled, and his defiance of the natural order.

Little brothers are not meant to win over their older brothers. When this does happen, there is usually a price to pay. In Shakespeare's *The Tempest*, Antonio usurps his older brother Prospero's dukedom, and is duly punished by the gods for his unnatural behaviour. Ironically, he is shipwrecked on the same island where Prospero has been imprisoned. Will this be Ed Miliband's fate?

Freud first described man's unconscious desire to kill the father in order to step into his shoes in his essay *Totem and Taboo*. The guilt evoked by this unconscious murderous rivalry is what, according to Freud, establishes cohesion within the group. It is the glue that binds a community together and enables it to function in a healthy way and to accept authority.

The Oedipal guilt that Freud traced to its evolutionary roots was driven by the son's desire to possess the mother, his first love object, and to supplant the father. However, the sibling rivalry we have witnessed between the Miliband brothers has a different objective. It is not a fight to replace the father; it is a fight to be first in their father's love—to have the birthright of the firstborn.

In the Biblical story of Jacob and Esau, Jacob is born fast on the heels of his twin brother Esau. When the time comes for their father, Isaac, who is nearing death, to bestow his blessing upon Esau, Jacob grabs the opportunity. With his mother's help, Jacob disguises himself before his blind father, Isaac, in order to steal his older brother's birthright. The name Jacob, in Hebrew, means "heel-catcher" or "supplanter".

Unlike Jacob and Esau, Ed and David are not twins—David is three years older—and Ed claims he has no memory of fighting with his brother as children. Nevertheless, both sons grew up under the powerful influence of their socialist/Marxist father, Ralph Miliband, who, as a Belgian Jew fleeing from the Nazi scourge, was a strong supporter of political activism and the Labour Party.

Family dinners centred around political debate and socialist principles. While David has been described as more of his father's intellectual heir, Ed preferred to sneak off to watch the soap opera *Dallas* on television. Ed's fascination with the dynastic battles of the Ewing family may have served as a foretaste of his own family battle.

Ed has shown considerable admiration for both his father and his brother and has enjoyed the reputation of being considered the "nicer" of the two brothers, being more "person-oriented", as opposed to David's cooler focus on policy-making. Ed has also followed more closely in his father's socialist footsteps, promoting fairness and social equality, supporting the unions, and eschewing private-sector input in education.

But behind Ed's "nice" persona, a much more ruthless politician has emerged who, like Jacob, took advantage of an opportunity to oust his brother. Also, just as Jacob had the support of his mother, Ed remembers his mother saying to him at bedtime, "Are you a boy to go tiger-shooting with?" He was being primed for the kill— and for winning the approval of both his mother and his father.

David, on the other hand, does not see his parents as pushing their children to succeed. He has said: "For families of the post-Holocaust generation, there were generally two responses: one guilt, that you are alive, two, so much guilt that you had to be at the top of the class always. My parents didn't fall into either of those attitudes. They held the belief simply that there were great blessings to being born in 1960s London compared to 1930s Poland, where my mother started out, or being in occupied Belgium, and that was something they were determined to make the most of for their boys."

Nevertheless, what seems to have been emphasised within the ethos of the family was the importance of taking advantage of the opportunities presented to them as a way of combating the losses of the past and surviving the threats of the future.

As the younger son who was in David's intellectual shadow, Ed's success may have been especially determined by spotting the right moment to compete. As Ed admitted, "The biggest obstacle to me standing was undoubtedly that I knew David would be against me. I genuinely made the decision after the election … And what it came down to was this: am I really going to say I am not going to stand because my brother is standing? If he wasn't in the race, I would not have had any hesitation. And in the end politics is about seizing the moment."

But, having seized the moment and having killed his tiger, Ed must now bear the inevitable guilt of succeeding over his brother, while David has to face the reconstruction of his role as the older brother who has been defeated. Upon hearing the election results, Ed made a point of embracing his brother, pounding his back repeatedly, while David maintained a painfully stiff smile.

Ed has made it clear that he will give his brother any job he wants, declaring: "I love you so much as a brother". As Freud recognised in *Totem and Taboo*, it is the power of guilt that will bind the two brothers most closely together.

The problem, however, that lies ahead for Ed is that as long as he succumbs to his guilt, David will be the albatross that he carries around his neck. In order to fully succeed without encumbrance, Ed will either have to be even more ruthless and plan a future without his brother, or one of them will have to leave the political field altogether and succeed in another arena—just as Jacob and Esau had to establish their own separate nations.

Although the extent of the damage that has been done to David's political career is not yet evident, Ed now faces the inevitable challenge of what he chooses to do with his guilt. Like Antonio stranded on Prospero's island, Ed and David remain bound together—but for how long?

27 September 2010

55

Does Julian Assange suffer from being a mama's boy?

The boy with an "enormous ego" and an adoring mother

In anticipation of their reunion last week, Christine Assange, Julian Assange's fifty-nine-year-old mother, declared, "I can't wait to see my son and to hold him close." Christine Assange arrived in London from her home in Australia while her son was still being held in solitary confinement in Wandsworth Prison. After seeing him, she said, "I'm connected back with him again. I've got the connection."

Now released on bail, Julian Assange, his mother, and his entourage are spending Christmas together at the Suffolk manor house belonging to Vaughan Smith, journalist and founder of the Frontline Club.

It is clear that Christine Assange feels close to her son. But does the connection between mother and son hold clues to explain his obsession with computer hacking, with exposing secret information, and with the allegations of sexual assault made against him following a trip to Sweden in August?

Julian Assange never knew his father, whose identity remains unknown. What is known is that his mother had been fleeing from a former lover whom she said had been stalking her. Christine Assange's peripatetic lifestyle had only just begun.

A year after Julian's birth, Christine married Brett Assange, the director of a theatre touring company, and the family moved constantly throughout Julian's childhood. By the time Julian was fourteen, he had lived in thirty-seven different towns, changing schools and sometimes being home-schooled.

Brett Assange recalls that his step-son was a "gifted child with an enormous ego", and that he was "deliberately treated like an adult" by his parents. He also remembers how Julian was often bullied at school for being a "nerd" and at a very young age was fascinated by equipment, taking it apart and putting it back together.

"Strangely enough", Brett Assange admits, "I always thought he would do something like this. He was always very independent and he certainly wouldn't take no for an answer."

By the time Julian was eight, his mother had re-married and gave birth to his half-brother. Three years later, in 1982, this marriage broke up and a custody battle ensued that prompted Christine Assange to go into hiding for the next five years with her sons.

The only stable factor in Julian Assange's early life was his mother. The fact that his mother's relationships with men tended to be fraught with conflict might have also made it difficult for her son to feel close to men or to identify with them positively.

At the age of eighteen, Julian fathered a son, Daniel, with a seventeen-year-old girl. They set up house together, and it was during this time that Julian learned to hack into computers and the internet. In October 1991, their house in Melbourne was raided by the police and he was subsequently charged with offences relating to computer hacking. His girlfriend fled with Daniel.

Shortly after their separation, Julian became severely depressed and was hospitalised for six months. History repeated itself. The couple embarked on a nine-year custody dispute that was settled in 1999, giving the mother sole responsibility for Daniel's upbringing.

Given this background, it would hardly be surprising if mother and son did not have a strong connection, especially during their years of hiding, but also perhaps in Julian's early childhood. His step-father's reference to his "enormous ego" suggests a child who felt that the world revolved around him, a "golden boy" idealised by his mother and "treated like an adult".

Although Julian Assange took his name from his step-father, there seems to have been no real father present in his life. Added to this was a vulnerable mother, needing protection from men, and the young Assange must have found himself in an impossible psychological corner.

Never having known his father, Julian may well have felt rejected by him, angry about the way he had treated his mother (at least in his mind), and possibly angry for leaving him to look after his mother. It is striking that Brett Assange admits that he went along with his wife in deliberately treating Julian "like an adult", suggesting that he did not assume a paternal role towards his step-son and was unable to provide that security for him.

Without parents who were able to set limits and recognise their son's vulnerability, there was no stopping Julian's omnipotent behaviour. As Brett Assange said, "He certainly wouldn't take no for an answer".

When we are infants, we all experience ourselves as the centre of the universe. This illusion of omnipotence is necessary psycho-logically to protect ourselves from overwhelming experiences of helplessness and vulnerability, and it is also necessary in establish-ing a core sense of self that is later modified by the limitations of external reality.

When the mother idolises her child, this early experience of omnipotence remains unmediated and the child's narcissistic bond to the mother is not broken. Mother and son continue to harbour an exclusive relationship from which the father is absent. This can lead in some cases to homosexual disturbances, with the son either turning to men as sexual partners or having fleeting relationships with women, as a way of defending against being engulfed by the mother.

Julian Assange's life's work has been to hack his way into the secrets of the internet, expose these secrets, and in doing this to attack and attempt to destroy the reputation of established authority figures. Whatever we may think of WikiLeaks and the role it plays in uncovering global injustices, it is clear that Julian Assange is out to attack the father in the form of government and corporate authority.

Assange is also facing *allegations of sexual assault* where he is being accused of forcing two women to have unprotected sex. His apparent inability to accept a "no" from these women reveals not only a refusal to allow anything to get in the way of his desire to possess and control women, but also suggests a lack of respect for women.

In an *interview* yesterday with John Humphrys on the *Today* programme, Assange explained, "... they found out that they were mutual former lovers of mine and that they had had unprotected sex and they got into a tizzy about whether there was a possibility of sexually transmitted disease". He went on to say, "It was a ridiculous thing to go to the police about".

Assange's fascination for exposing secrets can be likened to the desire to enter the forbidden zone of the parents' bedroom, to steal the magical phallus of the father, and to come between the couple. A journalist recently recounted meeting Assange at a restaurant in Sweden. The journalist was accompanied by his girlfriend.

Assange and the girlfriend went outside to smoke and when the journalist followed them outside to see what was keeping them, he could see Assange whispering in her ear. When the journalist challenged Assange, "He dropped into a classic fighter's pose with his fists up". Assange subsequently seduced the girlfriend to spend the night with him. As the journalist commented, "Assange seemed to take pleasure in humiliating me".

While asserting his innocence, Assange accuses others around him of abusing power. He refers to an "espionage indictment made secretly against me in the US", of "investigations conducted in secret", and of a "smear campaign" launched against him. His accusations display a paranoia that only confirms his anxiety that his own attacks are being turned against him. Father is fighting back. He can then become the martyr son who is abused by the father—a hero and a victim at the same time.

But in considering these attempts to usurp the father in order to regain exclusive possession of the mother, we come back to the question of Assange's relationship with women. In his desire for unprotected sex, Assange is asserting his right to impregnate women—even against their will. But these are not women he has a serious relationship with. Like his unknown father, he too will presumably disappear.

Is this his attempt to turn the tables and to wreak revenge on the mother who loved him and left him? This may also explain Assange's breakdown when his girlfriend and mother of his son left him after his arrest. The trauma of this abandonment may have reverberated with an earlier trauma of being adored and then betrayed by his mother.

Is Assange caught in some unconscious enactment that is tragically leading him to self-destruction? He models himself as a hero fighting injustice, but the real injustice may very well be buried in his psyche.

22 December 2010

56

Why the world will weep for Nelson Mandela

His impending death is especially sad not because he was perfect—but because he tried so hard

"There is no passion to be found in playing small—in settling for a life that is less than the one you are capable of living." These words of Nelson Mandela could not ring more true as he lies in hospital in Pretoria, gravely ill, and we look back on his life and legacy.

Readmitted on Saturday with a recurring lung infection, the former president, now ninety-four, is reported to be in a serious but stable condition. The headlines over the weekend spoke of South Africa and the world "holding its breath". There is a sense that we are about to witness an outpouring of grief the likes of which are rarely seen.

Mandela's impending death crystallises both his significance and our loss. Winner of the Nobel Peace Prize and long-term prisoner in his fight against South Africa's apartheid, Mandela is not only thought of as Father ("Tata") to black South Africans but as one of the outstanding heroes of the last century.

Along with Martin Luther King and Mahatma Gandhi, he was an inspirational leader whose personal and political life appeared seamless. His life and work have come to represent the global struggle for human dignity, equality, and democracy.

While the struggle is never-ending, Mandela reminds us that it is a struggle worth having.

Mandela's fight has had international repercussions. Many of the Britons who will mourn him will have memories of marching in London against apartheid, or boycotting the sale of South African oranges at Sainsbury's. They will recall vividly the day in February 1990 when they sat glued to their television sets, awaiting his release from prison. When he finally emerged, smiling and punching the air in a victory salute, one sensed unseen millions punching the air in unison.

Later, he spearheaded the Truth and Reconciliation Commission, which became a model for how to acknowledge human rights violations, create restorative justice, and set the historical record straight—all in a spirit of dignity rather than retribution.

These were some of his many achievements. This does not mean they were lasting ones. Inter-racial conflicts remain unresolved. The Truth and Reconciliation Commission has been accused of letting crimes go unpunished.

The heroic enterprise is by its very nature one that is necessarily doomed because in the end it is human. The role of the hero is to set an example of what we can ideally strive for—to be the best we can be—and ultimately to show us, through his failings, that we remain human and must struggle with our own individual and collective destructiveness.

For Mandela, racism was not simply a black/white issue. His greatness was to recognise that racism is rooted in the way we relate to others who are different from ourselves and whom we readily transform into enemies.

Freud refers to this process as the "narcissism of minor differences". This means that we defend our sense of identity by treating those who are different as "other", and often as sub-human, projecting all the inferior qualities we most despise in ourselves onto those who are "other" than us. According to Freud, this is part of the human condition. It is the destructive side of our nature—our tragic flaw.

Paradoxically, it is Mandela's failure to achieve absolute lasting peace that has also marked his efforts as heroic. His life's struggle has shone a spotlight on both the best and worst of what it means to be human.

Most important, he leaves us with an abiding truth about how we relate to others and how we relate to the bits of ourselves that we most abhor. In Mandela's words, "If you want to make peace with your enemy, you have to work with your enemy. Then he becomes your partner." Hope is dying; long live hope.

10 June 2013

57

Criado-Perez scare: what turns men into misogynist bullies?

As another man is arrested, a psychoanalyst's take on why men today might feel insecure and attack women

"A woman, especially, if she have the misfortune of knowing anything, should conceal it as well as she can." This advice comes from Jane Austen's *Pride and Prejudice*. The year was 1813. Not much has changed—or has it?

Now Jane Austen is to grace our £10 notes thanks to the persuasiveness of Caroline Criado-Perez, who argued that we need another woman, apart from the Queen, to appear on our banknotes. (Winston Churchill had been the favoured option.)

But the Bank's decision to accept her argument has triggered a wave of social media misogynist bullying, initially aimed at Criado-Perez, and rapidly spreading to prominent women who have taken her side. They have received threats of *rape and death*.

So what has changed since Austen cautioned women to keep a low profile? And why are we seeing an outburst of virulent hatred towards women now?

Animosity between the sexes is nothing new. Noting the anxiety caused by the perception of difference between the sexes, Freud coined the phrase "narcissism of minor differences" in his 1917 essay *The Taboo of Virginity*. Hatred of difference—of "otherness"—is embedded in our psyches and only mitigated by our need for the other. The anxiety caused by otherness is that it is something unknown and beyond our control.

When we feel secure, someone who is "other" is less threatening and becomes attractive *because* he or she is different. However, when our identity is under threat, the opposite is the case and the "other", who we once loved, can suddenly turn into an object of hatred.

Women are, by and large, used to being dependent in some way on men. For men, it is more complex. Every man has experienced total dependency on his mother at the start of life and, as a normal part of growing up, struggles to separate and become independent from his mother.

When there are difficulties in separating, or when early dependency is not safe, men may well fear their dependency on women in later life. This is manifest in the macho man who tries to ward off his vulnerability by being super-strong.

When men feel undermined or insecure, the first target for their frustrations is often women—especially when they perceive women to be in a stronger position or when they are actually dependent on them.

And there are plenty of reasons why men might feel insecure in today's Britain.

Long-term unemployment has hit a seventeen-year high, with its greatest impact on men. An increasing number of jobs are filled by women. Among university graduates, women in the UK outnumber and outperform men.

Marriage is also on the decline, and there is an increase in single-parent families, mostly headed by women. The only part of the economy in which men are doing better than women is at the top end, or corporate level, where the "glass ceiling" has hardly cracked.

Apart from wartime, when women filled in for men in the job market, these demographics are showing us that something is in fact radically changing in our society. Many men are feeling redundant.

Against this backdrop, internet misogyny is like a volcanic rumble that tells us some seismic shift is afoot in our social structure. Although most of us would agree that it is beneficial for women to have more opportunities and advantages than they've had in the past, we have naively failed to consider the downside of this and what it means in particular to male–female relations.

When economies change, social structures change. In the war-torn Democratic Republic of Congo, where entire villages on the northeast border with Rwanda have been decimated, most of the surviving men have lost their livelihoods and rely on their wives or women relatives to provide for them (for example, through the cultivation of food). While this has given women much greater economic power and independence, it has also created domestic tension as roles are reversed and men are left at home unemployed. One result of this has been a marked increase in domestic violence. As men feel emasculated, they try to regain an illusion of power through violence.

Is this what we are seeing in the trolls who are attacking women in the media—a kind of widespread domestic violence protected by the anonymity of Twitter? The stirrings of a gender crisis?

Although Britain is not at war, the current recession, along with the increasing demand within the job market for women and for "female" skills—for example, to listen and to put others first—is causing role reversals that we have rarely seen before on such a large scale. For many middle- and working-class men who are facing greater unemployment and poorer education prospects, being in such a vulnerable position is painful.

One way to get rid of these feelings is to attack the "other"—the women—who are threatening their security. The misogynist trolls seem to be ferociously trying to push their own fear and vulnerability onto their women victims—much like passing a hot potato. Hatred and denigration of the "weaker" sex makes trolls feel superior—they feel themselves to be the powerful ones, not vice versa.

The violent language and threats this has produced is shocking. But the emasculation that it points to and how we think about gender, the structure of the family, and child-rearing in our changing society is the volcano waiting to erupt.

Is Jane Austen looking down on us with a bit of a raised eyebrow as we await her debut on the £10 note?

7 August 2013

Ed Miliband and the problems of being Ralph's heir apparent

Does Ed's victory over his brother have a bearing on his fight to defend his father's reputation?

ED MILIBAND is no stranger to being attacked in public. On a walkabout in August in Walworth's East Street Market, he laughed off the egg that was dripping down the side of his head, thanking the market for his warm welcome and the "easy availability of eggs".

Last Saturday the *Daily Mail* threw a rotten egg at Miliband's socialist father, Ralph. In his article, "*The Man Who Hated Britain*", Geoffrey Levy portrayed Miliband senior as fundamentally anti-British, suggesting his Marxist views were "fuelled by a giant-size social chip on his shoulder as he lived in his adoptive country". Levy then tarnished Miliband Jnr for paying homage to his father's Marxism by pledging to bring back socialism.

The truth, as many commentators have pointed out, is that it is more likely that Ralph Miliband would turn in his grave if he knew the nature of the socialism his son is promoting.

This time, however, Ed Miliband has thrown the egg back, accusing the *Daily Mail* of publishing "an appalling lie" about his father.

While it may be considered below the belt to attack a politician by smearing his father's reputation, isn't this part of the slings and arrows of politics—especially when the father in question was such an important public figure? Obviously, Ed Miliband disagrees. This was an egg too far and it seems to have hit a sore spot.

In his *rebuttal*, published in the *Daily Mail*, he castigated Levy for "overstepping" the boundaries of decency and civilised debate by "besmirching and undermining" his father.

He sought to set the record straight on his father's love of the country that effectively saved the lives of both his Jewish refugee parents and enabled the family to flourish intellectually and materially. He also made it clear that he has taken a "different path" from his father politically, emphasising that his loyalty to his father is filial rather than intellectual.

Is this a simple story of a son defending his father? Or does Ed Miliband's quest to honour his father reflect a more complex family dynamic?

There is no doubt that both Miliband sons had a close relationship with their father and that political debate was at the core of family life. During a teaching stint in the United States, Ralph Miliband wrote to Ed, his younger son: "If anyone else read this, and did not know the way we talk, or you talk, they would think I was crazy to be writing this to a twelve-year-old boy—but I know better, and find it very nice."

This closeness may have easily instilled in the young Ed both a desire to fulfill his father's vision and a conflict in disagreeing with this vision. By the time of Ralph Miliband's death in 1994, on the cusp of Tony Blair's takeover of the Labour Party, both David and Ed had embarked on political careers aligning themselves with what was to become New Labour. David worked for Tony Blair, while Ed worked for Gordon Brown. David in particular had established himself in a different camp.

Both sons were beginning to pave the way for the sibling contest that eventually led to Ed's victory in the Labour leadership race.

Damian McBride, spin doctor to Gordon Brown, claims that it was Ed's obsession with the legacy of his father—rather than his rivalry with his brother—that spurred him to challenge David, a Blairite, to the party leadership. This might suggest that Ed had a closer bond to his father than his brother did.

On the other hand, David was described as his father's intellectual heir and this might have well been a thorn in Ed's side.

Whatever favouritism might have taken place in the Miliband family, Ed's vigorous public defence of his father makes it clear that his father is his territory. It is striking that neither David nor their mother, Marion Kozak, has made any public statement.

The debacle with the *Daily Mail* has provided a platform on which Ed can declare himself as heir apparent to his father—but an heir who is also candidly critical of the old order. In the background is Ed's victory over his brother and whatever residual guilt he may feel about this. Does this additional guilt make it even more important for him to profess his allegiance to his father?

And how could this play out in the upcoming general election campaign? How will Ed steer his way through trying to please the ghost of his father and at the same time compete with him? Strong bonds are needed to withstand a victory over brother and father.

3 October 2013